The Texas Divorce Handbook:

Your Step-by-Step Guide to Successfully Navigating Texas Divorce

By: Bryan Fagan, ESQ.

The Texas Divorce Handbook:
Your Step-by-Step Guide to
Successfully Navigating Texas Divorce

By: Bryan Fagan, ESQ.

"A journey of a thousand miles begins with a single step." ~Lao-
Tzu

This Texas Divorce Handbook is your step-by-step guide to successfully navigating Texas divorce. Use it accordingly—mark it up, fold down the pages, highlight important topics, make notes in the margins, and pass it along to a friend in need. Use it as it was intended to be used – as a guide to those in search of answers.

Do NOT, however, allow this book to take the place of consulting an actual Texas divorce lawyer and sharing the specific facts and circumstances of your situation. Nothing can take the place of a live consultation with a knowledgeable attorney.

Therefore, I'm offering a free consultation with an attorney at my law firm, a $350 value, to encourage you to find the answers you need to navigate toward a successful future.

Call our office today:

(281) 717-6711

www.bryanfagan.com

Call or click to make your appointment for a FREE 60-MINUTE consultation today

– A $350 Value –

For additional information contact:

Bryan Fagan

Law Office of Bryan Fagan

17101 Kuykendahl Road,

Houston, TX 77068

Tel: (281) 717-6711

Fax: (855) 668-0536

www.bryanfagan.com

FIRST EDITION

ISBN-13: 978-0692861424 (Law Office of Bryan Fagan)

ISBN-10: 0692861424

Legal Disclaimer

This Book is Not Legal Advice

While this book provides a good amount of legal information, the intent is that it is to be used strictly for review and educational purposes only. This information is in no way intended to be interpreted as legal advice about any particular situation. You should seek the advice of an attorney before acting on any of the information provided. There is no substitute for legal advice from a qualified, licensed attorney.

TABLE OF CONTENTS

INTRODUCTION

I have been encouraged to write a book at more times in my life than I can recall. The reality was that I did not want to write a book. Why not? Because, I did not believe I could find the time in my busy work and family life schedule. What I do have in my possession, however, are numerous blog posts, most of which are about family law and divorce. These blogs include information that can help prepare individuals who are contemplating a divorce for the challenges they will face prior to, during, and after the divorce process. So rather than write a book, I decided to aggregate, curate, and update some of my most popular blog posts from the past few years.

As you go through this collection, don't feel you have to read it like a book. Use it as a reference to prepare yourself for the process, and then use it as something you can go back to when you need it. Scan it and find the posts that relate to you during the different stages of the process, or read every single word of every post. However you approach this book, I hope you will find a nugget or three that will help you reach and achieve your goals.

Are you contemplating divorce, but have no clue where to begin? Did your spouse already have you served with a citation and an Original Petition for Divorce? Are you seriously concerned with protecting your rights? Do you know how custody will be decided for your children? If you have questions like these and others, then this book is the ideal place to begin your Texas divorce education.

To successfully launch your divorce education, the information in this book has been organized in a way to introduce you to each phase of the divorce process.

Chapter One: Fifteen Steps to Take When Preparing for your Divorce lists 15 things you should consider doing as you prepare to seek a divorce in Texas.

Chapter Two: Six Tips Before You Meet with A Divorce Lawyer provides additional information on getting ready for a divorce and in particular how you can prepare to meet with a divorce lawyer to maximize your time and get your questions answered.

Chapter Three: Nine Questions to Ask Yourself and the Divorce Lawyer Before You Hire One helps you figure out how to choose a divorce attorney to represent you. This may be the most important step in your case. It is important to be selective. I'll explain what characteristics you should look for in an attorney before you make a hiring decision.

Your future and the future of your children will depend in great part on the counsel you choose to represent your interests and protect your rights.

Chapter Four: Texas Divorce Basics introduces you to the basic process and the key issues in Texas divorce. Many people believe a divorce is a simple matter of filling out some forms and changing their status from married to single. However, it's much more than that.

Chapter Five: Can I get a Legal Separation or Common Law Divorce? answers two of the questions I get asked most frequently during my consult.

Chapter Six: Common Law Marriage and Texas Divorce introduces people to the basic concepts of common-law marriage and how it may be relevant in your divorce. Also discussed is what it takes to meet the Texas statutory requirements of a common-law marriage.

Chapter Seven: How Long Will My Texas Divorce Take? discusses another frequently asked question in my divorce consult "How soon can I be divorced?"

Chapter Eight: How Much Will My Texas Divorce Cost? discusses the cost of a divorce. Although there is no single answer, I tackle the question and provide a guestimate based on different possible scenarios and depending on how far down the divorce path a case travels.

Chapter Nine: Eight Tips for Reducing the Cost of a Divorce provides tips to help guide you in reducing the costs of a Texas Divorce.

Chapter Ten: How am I Going to Pay for My Texas Divorce? discusses various methods that some people have utilized to pay for the services of a divorce lawyer when money was not readily available.

Chapter Eleven: Does it Matter Who Files First in a Texas Divorce discusses the concern of many potential clients regarding whether filing first in their divorce case matters. For many there is an impression that if they are not the first to file, they will be at a disadvantage in their case.

Chapter Twelve: Steps for Filing for Divorce in Texas discusses the next step after hiring a divorce lawyer and what is involved in initiating a divorce in Texas and the documents that will be filed with the court. You will read about the different things that go into the documents. The documents are a roadmap for divorce. They are an overview of what you are asking and give you a bird's-eye view of what to expect.

Chapter Thirteen: Service of Process explains how a spouse is brought under the power of the court and how it is required under the Texas Family Code that a spouse be notified when a divorce case has been opened. The different methods of service are explained.

Chapter Fourteen: What does a Default Judgment Mean in a Texas Divorce? discusses what can happen when the person who was served with the divorce paperwork fails to file a written answer with the court within the required time.

Chapter Fifteen: How to Draft and File an Answer to a Texas Divorce provides the necessary information and steps that can be taken after being served with divorce paperwork to prevent a default judgment. Doing nothing will result in your ex being able to default you for divorce. Your first step is to put together a response to their

Original Petition for Divorce.

Chapter Sixteen: Preparing your Divorce Case for Mediation answers common questions regarding why mediation is important and if mediation is required. It also discusses why it is important and ways you can prepare your case for mediation.

Chapter Seventeen: The Divorce Temporary Orders handles one of the biggest concerns spouses have after filing for divorce, which is, "What happens now?" If mediation is unsuccessful in resolving a divorce case on a final or temporary basis, the next step is to go to court for a Temporary Orders hearing.

Chapter Eighteen: Getting Ready for a Temporary Orders Hearing answers common questions that many people have regarding a temporary orders hearing, and gives you an idea of what to expect when preparing for the hearing and when you testify.

Chapter Nineteen: Child Custody Basics in Texas covers the basic information you need to know regarding planning for child custody in a divorce. I discuss conservatorship, visitation, rights and duties, child support, and parenting plans. I have included a segment on the Standard Possession Order, along with some very important custody tips on what to do and what not to do.

Chapter Twenty: Dividing Property in a Texas Divorce covers the division of property. To understand how assets and debts are divided in the divorce, you will need to understand the distinction between separate property and community property.

Chapter Twenty-One: Alimony, When is it Available in a Texas Divorce? addresses Spousal Support, Spousal Maintenance, and Alimony in Texas and when they are available.

Chapter Twenty-Two: What is Discovery and Why do I need to do it? discusses how discovery is an important tool in gathering the needed information to prove your case.

Chapter Twenty-Three: When Should You Go to Divorce Court in Texas? explains that there are two good reasons for going to divorce court in Texas: (1) To have a prove-up hearing for an agreed-upon divorce or (2) When an agreement cannot be reached with a difficult spouse.

Chapter Twenty-Four: Six Things You Need to Know Before You Divorce includes six recommended actions to take before proceeding with a divorce. These steps are specific to a Texas divorce, but can be applied to a divorce in many states. It is important to be certain that you have done everything you need to do in order to feel right about the outcome.

Chapter Twenty-Five: Do NOT Make This Decision by Yourself! encourages the readers of the book not to proceed without consulting with an attorney. Readers are also provided with a free gift to help facilitate their taking the next step.

Chapter Twenty-Six: About the Author—Bryan Fagan, Esq. provides the reader a little information regarding the author of the book.

CHAPTER 1

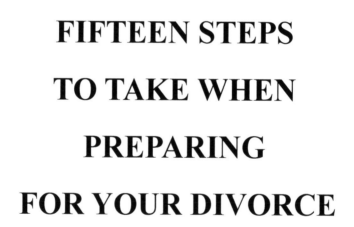

FIFTEEN STEPS
TO TAKE WHEN
PREPARING
FOR YOUR DIVORCE

I have written several articles regarding considerations to make when preparing for a divorce in Texas on my blog. However, this question comes up a lot in my consultations so I thought I would take some time and write a little bit more on the subject for this book.

1. CHANGE PASSWORDS AND PIN NUMBERS ON ALL YOUR ACCOUNTS

It is important to properly protect yourself. As soon as you know you will be filing for divorce, change every one of your passwords to something that your spouse will not be able to guess. If you are one of those people that only uses 2-3 passwords for everything, think of something new, preferably using random letters and numbers. This should include changing PIN numbers on your debit cards and the passwords on all your bank account websites.

2. HAVE MONEY SET ASIDE THAT YOUR SPOUSE DOES NOT HAVE ACCESS TO

A divorce can be very expensive. Often during the divorce process, one spouse cannot access funds to move ahead with their divorce because the other spouse controls all access to the marital funds. This puts the other spouse at a great disadvantage in terms of hiring professionals to navigate the divorce as well as having sufficient money to live on. Taking steps ahead of time can help get you to the point in the divorce process that will secure child support or possible spousal support.

3. GET A NEW MAILING ADDRESS

It is important to protect your communications during the divorce. Sometimes a spouse will be able to intercept your mail. Should this happen, it will not only hinder your ability to gather the information your lawyer needs; it may interfere with your lawyer's ability to communicate with you. One possible solution would be to establish a P.O. box and have your mail forwarded to the P.O. box. Taking this preventive measure will save you a great deal of future heartache.

4. OBTAIN A SEPARATE EMAIL ADDRESS

If you share an email address with your spouse, it is time to get your own. There are multiple free email providers to choose from including Gmail, Yahoo, Outlook, etc. It is not recommended that you use your work email. Under the law, your employer owns that email and may be subject to a subpoena from your spouse's attorney, meaning your ex can then get access to all of your work emails.

5. OBTAIN A COPY OF YOUR CREDIT REPORT

Some of my clients have discovered their spouse has used their name and credit to secure loans, credit cards, etc. without telling my client about it first. Obtaining a credit report will allow you to find out about any unknown debts earlier rather than later. There are many internet sites available where you can obtain a free copy of your credit report.

6. TAKE STEPS TO PROTECT YOUR CREDIT

One of the first things you should consider prior to filing for divorce is to remove your spouse as an authorized user from your credit cards. Authorized user means your spouse is not responsible to the lender for the debt that is incurred but they are able to charge on the account. Enrolling in free credit monitoring services will also alert you to changes on your credit report to help you spot any possibly incorrect information on your report. You may want to watch out for accounts you never opened and hard inquiries placed by creditors with whom you have not applied for credit.

7. IF POSSIBLE, AT LEAST PAY THE MINIMUM AMOUNT ON FINANCIAL OBLIGATIONS

It can be financially difficult to carry the full cost of a monthly mortgage payment, credit card payments, and other financial obligations by yourself. It may be tempting to stop paying when you are not getting any help from your spouse. Not paying can hurt your credit score and may cause you to be in default on your mortgage, eventually leading to the lender repossessing your home. Losing your home could be painful and lead to the loss of any home equity you may have acquired.

8. USE A CALENDAR

A calendar and accurate timeline of events may become an important tool in your divorce. You will need something to keep track of visits you or your spouse have with your children, incidents between you and your spouse, appointments with your attorney, or court dates. This can be a physical calendar, an app on your phone, or a simple word document.   If you use a smartphone, you can also use the calendar/notes app on the phone. It is important to be aware that if you back up your phone "to the cloud" and if you share a user account with your spouse, they may be able to access your notes. Refer back to numbers 1 & 4 on this list; change all your passwords.

9. CHANGE YOUR BENEFICIARIES AND GET A NEW WILL

One of the conversations I have with my clients during the divorce process is that they need to start thinking about changing their will and updating their beneficiaries with any and all financial institutions. One the questions I ask my clients is, "If you died today, do you want your spouse to get everything?" Most of the time, the answer is no. If you do not have a will, you should get at least a simple will. If you die without a will before the divorce is final, your spouse will probably inherit most of your estate.

10. TAKE A LOOK AT YOUR SOCIAL MEDIA PROFILES

The deletion of pictures and posts from your social media account, during or prior to litigation, could be deemed to be destruction of evidence for which you could be sanctioned by the court. However, many accounts such as Facebook will allow you to deactivate the account with the ability to reactivate if necessary.

11. UNTANGLE JOINT ACCOUNTS IF POSSIBLE

Many married couples share joint bank accounts, which means both parties have equal access to the accounts. Nevertheless, people regularly come into my office and are surprised to find that their spouse has raided the account. One of these incidents stands out in my mind. On that occasion, I remember overhearing a client who was signing up saying to one of my paralegals, "Bryan asked me has your wife cleaned out your bank account yet? I told Bryan she would never do that. When I went home she was gone, and then I looked online, and I saw there was nothing in our checking account."

12. DO NOT LEAVE YOUR SPOUSE WITH NOTHING

My advice to my clients is not to do what this wife did to her husband, but to protect yourself by opening a separate account and withdrawing no more than one-half of the proceeds of the joint accounts to give you something to live on for a while. Keep in mind that if you withdraw the entire account, a judge will be scrutinizing these actions later in court. It is one thing to protect yourself; it is another thing to leave your wife and children without any money to live on or buy food. It is usually a good idea to open the account at a different bank than the one at which you and your spouse have done business.

13. GET A COMPLETE PHYSICAL

There are several reasons to do this. One, divorce is one of the top five stressors you will ever go through, and it is more important than ever to make sure you stay healthy. Two, a person's physical health is an element considered by the court for numerous issues such as child custody and maintenance. Three, it is vital that you get yourself checked if you have any reason to suspect that your spouse has been unfaithful. If your spouse has infected you with a sexually transmitted disease, you need to find out before the divorce is over so your lawyer can ensure that the philanderer pays the expenses of treatment. I have had clients who have sought my services after finding out they had a sexually transmitted disease and the only source of that disease was their spouse.

14. IMMEDIATELY START GATHERING INFORMATION

It is important to start gathering admissible information for court. Often after a spouse finds out you are planning to divorce them, it becomes more difficult to find various financial documents. It is usually a good idea to obtain the following documents before your spouse knows you are seeking a divorce:

    A. Real estate closing documents – deeds, mortgages, notes, tax records, etc.

    B. Credit card statements

    C. Bank statements

    D. Loan documents

    E. Income tax returns (last 2 years)

    F. Paycheck stubs for both parties

G. Title statements

H. Investment account statements (Mutual funds, IRAs, stock certificates, etc.)

I. Retirement & pension account statements

J. Statements of insurance benefits (health, life, and disability)

Keep in mind that if there is a particular asset you believe to be non-marital, the burden is on you to prove that it is non-marital. If there is a certain document you cannot locate and you believe your spouse has it in his/her possession, tell your lawyer about it and he may be able to get it through the discovery process.

15. PLAN YOUR CUSTODY CASE

If you will seek primary custody of your children, you need to start planning your custody case immediately. One useful exercise is to think about how you will explain to the judge why you should have custody of your child. Write down everything you would say; get it all down on paper. What facts will need to be established with eye-witness testimony? Are there any facts that need documentary proof? Where can you find those documents? Bring this document with you when you visit with a lawyer. This will give your lawyer a chance to review things that you think are important and ask you any needed follow-up questions.

CHAPTER 2

SIX TIPS BEFORE YOU MEET WITH A DIVORCE LAWYER

After some consideration, you've decided to make one of the biggest decisions of your life and divorce your spouse. Whatever motivating factors led you to this choice, the fact remains that before you contact an attorney, it would be in your best interest to come prepared for any meeting with information and documents that are relevant to the process in which you and your family are about to become involved.

1) GENERAL INFORMATION

When I meet with a client, I tell them this is the "back of the baseball card" information: names, birthdays, social security numbers, date of the marriage, date the parties separated, information regarding the children of this marriage (and any previous marriages)—especially when those children are under 18 years old. The job you hold, the job your spouse holds, and your incomes are important when it comes to considerations of child and spousal support.

2) DAY-TO-DAY LIVING EXPENSES

This goes hand-in-hand with the income of each spouse that we just discussed. In order to make it through the divorce with minimal interruptions to the daily life of the parties and their children, it makes sense to let your attorney know all of the expenses each party has, their assets/liabilities, and a little bit about your own and your spouse's credit histories. If one party has an overwhelming amount of debt, your attorney should know about that immediately in order to plan ahead.

3) PROPERTY

Do you own the home you live in? Do you and your spouse own it jointly? These are bits of information that you attorney needs to have. Since Texas is a community property state, even if you bought your home prior to this marriage, your spouse may have a claim for reimbursement if the community income was utilized to make mortgage payments or improve the house. Another aspect of property to let your attorney know about immediately is if you and your spouse have agreed to the sale of a home or other property. The terms of your agreement can be ratified in the Final Decree of Divorce.

Personal property should be inventoried as well. Make a list of the major items in the home: furniture, electronics, art, jewelry, appliances, and contents of any safe(s) that you and your spouse own.

4) COPY DOCUMENTS

Tax filings, bank statements, statements from retirement accounts, and mortgage documents are just a few of the types of documents that are helpful for an attorney to have at the onset of the case. If there are files on the computer that you believe to be relevant, make copies and save them to a USB flash drive.

5) INFORMATION ON THE CHILDREN

Where do your kids go to school? What sort of extracurricular activities are they involved in? Do they have any "special needs" where they need to attend doctor's appointments or take medication on a regular basis? Begin to think about these subjects prior to going to see an attorney so that you can discuss your plan with an attorney. Parties will typically agree to one party being able to designate the primary residence of the kid(s) while the other can visit them with varying degrees of frequency. It is a best-case scenario when parties can agree to an arrangement whereby both can parent and be present for the children. However, when this is not possible, it is critical to let your attorney know of your situation and your desired outcome as far as the children are concerned.

6) QUESTIONS

Come prepared to ask your attorney questions about the process. I will typically initiate the "question session" during any meeting with a client, but if you have prepared questions to ask, it makes the discussion more fruitful and productive. The length of time of a divorce, details about selling a home after a divorce is finalized, visitation concerns, and community property are examples of questions that clients will ask with frequency.

Preparing a list of questions and pertinent information can be the basis of a strong attorney-client

relationship. A good Texas divorce lawyer will be able to help you organize your case in a way that will minimize stress and increase the chances of a successful and timely resolution.

Chapter 3

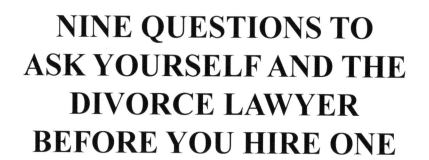

NINE QUESTIONS TO ASK YOURSELF AND THE DIVORCE LAWYER BEFORE YOU HIRE ONE

C hoosing an attorney to represent you in your family law matter may be one of the most important decisions you'll ever make. It is important to be selective when you are choosing a divorce attorney.

By doing so, you will be more confident about your representation throughout the legal proceedings. By choosing the right divorce lawyer for your case, you will increase your chances of obtaining the most favorable results for yourself and your children.

Although it important for you to understand how you will be charged, you should not base your hiring decision on cost alone. Some questions we encourage you to ask when hiring an attorney include:

1. DOES THE ATTORNEY OFFER A FREE CONSULTATION?

I have placed this one towards the top of the list. Although it is not the most important thing when it comes to hiring a divorce lawyer, it is an important tool for helping you to find the right attorney for your divorce case.

One of the best ways to choose a divorce lawyer is for you to interview attorneys. However, this can be a costly thing if the attorney charges a consultation fee. Attorney consultation fees can range from $150-$500/hour. This means if you interview three attorneys, you may have spent $450-$1,500 just interviewing lawyers *and the divorce has not even started yet.*

I (and several other divorce lawyers) offer free consultations. I do this in order to provide an opportunity to get to know prospective clients and for them to get to know me. This allows us both to find out if we will be able to work well together.

A question to ask yourself when you are interviewing divorce lawyers is do they provide you with sufficient information to help you make your decisions or do they hold back?

It is important for clients to have as much information as possible so they can make educated and informed decisions with attorney guidance.

Once the client makes the decision, it is the attorney's job to advocate for that decision. Some attorneys believe that they should make the decisions. It's your case and your life – you should make the decisions.

2. DO YOU FEEL COMFORTABLE WITH THE LAWYER?

I believe one of the most important requirements for choosing a divorce lawyer is that you need to feel comfortable with that lawyer. Some people have it in their heads that they need a "bulldog," or an attorney with 50 years of experience.

It is more important to have an attorney who is compatible with you and will listen to you, someone with whom you feel comfortable, someone who has a practice with a focus on divorce and family law, and most importantly, someone you can trust.

You need to believe in them and believe in their advice. If it takes several consultations to find that comfort level, then so be it. It is better to spend time up front finding a lawyer with whom you click than getting into court and not feeling like the person sitting next to you cares about you or your children.

3. WHAT ARE THE ATTORNEY'S CREDENTIALS AND IS THE LAW PRACTICE FOCUSED ON DIVORCE AND FAMILY LAW?

The most important thing to look for in selecting a divorce or family lawyer in Texas *is that they are licensed to practice in the state where the case is ongoing.*

I sometimes get clients who have a case in a state other than Texas. Unfortunately, depending on the circumstances, I may be unable to help them and need to refer them to an attorney licensed to practice in that state. Other times I can help them because the facts of their case are such that we can open a case in Texas and move forward.

The next important thing to look for is an attorney whose practice is focused on Divorce and Family Law. I sometimes run into attorneys who try and do all areas of the law. I believe this is a disservice to their clients. The one constant in the law is "change." Texas courts continue to interpret laws differently, and our Texas legislatures continue to pass new laws and change existing ones. The Texas rules of civil procedure, evidence, and local court rules vary from one judge to the next. All lawyers in the state of Texas are legally able to do divorce work, but you should look for someone who does only family law or for whom family law makes up most of their practice. They will be more likely aware of the latest changes in laws regarding the family.

It is important to look for a lawyer who has handled many divorce cases, has worked with complex asset divisions, has handled contested custody matters, and has been successful. That attorney will guide you through your divorce fluidly, efficiently, and competently.

My own office focuses exclusively on family law practice, including divorce, child custody, parenting establishment, and paternity. We have earned respect within the legal community for our trial skills, our knowledge of complex asset and property divisions, and our handling of child custody matters. We have been at this for many years, and we never lose sight of our clients' goals and needs. Whichever attorney you select should be similarly focused.

4. **HOW MUCH WILL THE LEGAL REPRESENTATION COST?**

Ask how much you will be charged for legal services and how much of an up-front fee is required. Find out what the attorney's billing practices are, because you need to know how and when you will be billed.

In family law, most attorneys charge an hourly rate. In the Houston, Texas area, this usually runs from $150 per hour to $500 per hour or more. At our office, we have several lawyers that bill at different rates. We can match you with one of our attorneys to help accommodate your budget.

Most the time we like to facilitate communications so if the client has a quick five-minute question, we will take and document the phone call on their invoice but not charge them. However, if this client calls us three or five times a day, then those calls will be lumped together and billed.

A normal case may have expenses and fees, such as filing fees, service fees, expert fees, or even document copying charges when documents are sent to a copier service. It is important to look at the fee agreement and see how you will be charged.

Some attorneys do not send out invoices to their clients for months at a time. Ask the attorney how they will bill their time on your case. Other law firms charge a minimum of 12 minutes for any task, regardless of whether the work required only three minutes. Furthermore, some firms charge a higher rate for appearing in court than the rate for other tasks.

Your attorney should help you become knowledgeable regarding the fee structure, and be able to help you make an informed decision.

5. **HAVE YOU EVER BEEN SANCTIONED FOR AN ATTORNEY ETHICS VIOLATION?**

Attorneys are held to high ethical standards regarding how they practice law and the customer service they provide to clients. The State Bar of Texas regulates its members and, when necessary, disciplines attorneys with sanctions to punish them for acts of professional misconduct.

A grievance filed against an attorney can lead to reprimand, probation, suspension, restitution, and revocation of the attorney's license to practice law within Texas. You need assurance that the character and competency of your attorney justifies your decision to hire. If you have concerns about an attorney, you can look them up on the Texas Bar Website.

6. WHAT KIND OF ONLINE REVIEWS DO THEY HAVE?

I am sometimes surprised when certain lawyers get hired. This is because a simple search online of the attorney's or firm's name would reveal either an ethics violation or that previous clients have had a bad experience with that attorney. Some places to check out a lawyer's reputation with clients includes Google, Yelp, or Avvo.

7. WILL I RECEIVE COPIES OF ALL DOCUMENTS IN MY CASE?

Ask how the attorney will ensure that you will have access to your documents whenever you need them. There can be nothing more worrisome than not knowing what has transpired in your case, or being asked to respond to a document in the case that you have never seen and know nothing about.

Unfortunately, some attorneys fail to provide their clients with copies of the documents filed with the court, orders issued by the court, or correspondence between the attorneys.

Our office copies clients on all communications with opposing parties and opposing counsel. This means if an email is sent to the other side, our attorneys and paralegals will copy you on those communications so you know what is being discussed.

If a document is filed with the court by our firm, we will send you a copy of that document. If we receive a document from an opposing counsel, we will forward you that document so you will have a chance to review it.

This is your case and you are entitled to know what is going on. It is our policy that you are always entitled to a copy of your file or anything in your file upon request.

8. HOW RESPONSIVE ARE YOU TO ANSWERING EMAILS AND RETURNING PHONE CALLS?

When you are looking for a divorce lawyer, one of the things you should consider is if you feel like the lawyer will be responsive to your needs and able to respond to your questions in a timely manner.

Some attorneys will not return your telephone calls within a reasonable time. Many attorneys struggle with communicating in a prompt manner with clients. Part of the problem for family law and divorce lawyers is due to the nature of their practice. They are out of the office more than many other types of lawyers. Divorce and Family Law Lawyers are often in Court or in Mediation, which means they are not in the office to answer calls and it can be difficult to respond promptly to emails for the same reason.

This can be especially difficult for attorneys who do not have a support staff to help them. The reality is that your attorney may not always be available as quickly as you like. He or she may be in court involved in another person's case and focused on that case. That is fine, because when it is your turn in court or mediation, you will want the attorney devoted to your case. A good question to ask prospective divorce and family law lawyers is how you will be able to contact them and how long it will take them to return your call.

9. HOW MUCH EXPERIENCE DO YOU HAVE WITH COMPLEX HIGH-ASSET PROPERTY DIVISIONS AND WITH FINDING HIDDEN ASSETS?

With some divorces, the property division may be complex and contentious. Adding to the tension is the reality that some spouses will attempt to conceal assets. Before deciding to hire a lawyer, you need to know whether the attorney is experienced in dealing with these matters.

When one party deliberately conceals assets, direct and swift action must be taken to bring those assets before the court for division. It is important to have a lawyer who has experience with high-asset divorce cases and knows how to search out clues to find hidden assets. Not all divorce attorneys have experience with business valuations, stock portfolios, finance matters, tax and debt issues, or how to uncover hidden assets.

Chapter 4

TEXAS DIVORCE BASICS

B efore deciding to proceed with a Texas divorce, it is a good idea to take time to understand the basic process and the key issues that must be addressed.

For most people, divorce is new and uncharted territory. It can be a frightening process. Obtaining information about the process can ease this anxiety considerably. In this chapter, we introduce and discuss the following concepts:

- Divorce and legal separation in Texas,

- The difference between a no-fault divorce, divorce with fault, and divorce from a covenant marriage,

- The difference between an uncontested divorce and contested divorce,

- The special characteristics of a military divorce,

- The availability of divorce self-help, and

- Continuing health insurance coverage under COBRA.

Divorce Terminates the Marriage Contract

From a legal standpoint, divorce is the method of terminating a marriage contract between two individuals (the parties). A divorce ends a valid marriage. It is the legal procedure that returns both parties to single status with the ability to remarry.

What many people do not know is that a divorce is a lawsuit that does more than end a marriage. A Texas Divorce takes care of three things:

1. **Children** – it gives both spouses the right to determine the future care and conservatorship of their children,

2. **Property and Debts** – it divides property and debts in a "just and right manner."

3. **Divorce** – Once the divorce is final, both parties are free to

marry someone new.

Divorce That's No One's Fault

A majority of states have at least one form of "no-fault" grounds for divorce. Texas is no exception and allows people to plead for divorce on "no-fault" grounds. This means a spouse can file for divorce under the grounds that the marriage has become insupportable.

This means a standard clause is placed in the Original Petition for Divorce that "the marriage has become insupportable because of a discord or conflict of personalities that destroys the legitimate ends of the marriage relationship." In other words, the spouse asking for the divorce wants a divorce.

What every spouse needs to know when pleading "no-fault" in a Texas divorce is that a divorce will be granted without either spouse alleging or having to prove marital fault, or guilt.

Meaning that for the purpose of the divorce itself, it is not necessary to prove fault under Section 6 of the Texas Family Code such as:

1. Living apart

2. Confinement in a mental hospital

3. Cruelty

4. Abandonment

5. Conviction of a felony

6. Adultery

Instead, one of the spouses must state under oath that "the marriage has become insupportable because of a discord or conflict of personalities that destroys the legitimate ends of the marriage relationship" with "no reasonable prospect of reconciliation."

Additionally, either spouse may obtain a divorce despite the other's objection. Mutual consent is not required for a no-fault divorce in Texas.

Divorce on Fault Grounds

As discussed above, Texas grants divorces based on the following fault grounds: adultery, cruelty, felony conviction, and abandonment.

In Texas, you can ask the court to give you the divorce because it was somebody's fault. If fault is proven, then when a court gives a divorce for "grounds," a court may give more of the community property to the "innocent" spouse.

Divorce from a Covenant Marriage

Texas does have fault grounds for a divorce that can be pled such as a spouse committing adultery. Usually this is done to try and get more property out of the divorce.

In some states, there is a type of marriage called a "Covenant Marriage," where similar legal grounds must be alleged to support a request for divorce from a covenant marriage.

Compared to a standard marriage, there are additional requirements for entering into a covenant marriage, such as premarital counseling. There are also specific statutory grounds for divorce from a covenant marriage.

Currently, Texas does not have a covenant marriage statute. In every legislative session, a bill is introduced to implement one, but as of this writing it has not passed.

Difference Between Contested and Uncontested Divorce

Before a divorce will be granted, there needs to be a clean slate. Matters of spousal maintenance, assignment of separate assets, division of community property and pensions, legal decision-making custody, parenting plans, and child support obligations must all be resolved.

In uncontested divorce in Texas, both spouses have reached an agreement on all divorce issues which include:

1. Both spouses agree to be divorced

2. Parental decision-making responsibilities for the children including such things as medical, educational and psychological decisions

3. Parental visitation

4. The amount and duration of child support

5. The amount and duration of any spousal support (alimony)

6. The division of property, and debts

If spouses can reach an agreement on all issues, it then becomes a matter of drafting the necessary paperwork, waiting the required period according to Texas law, proving up the divorce decree in court, and then the parties are divorced.

If spouses do not reach an agreement on all the basic issues, the divorce is then contested.

Residency Requirement

Under Texas Family Code Section 6.301, for a divorce action to be commenced in Texas Superior Court, one of the spouses must

have been domiciled in Texas for six months or more and a resident of the county in which the suit is filed for the preceding 90-day period.

This is a jurisdictional requirement, without which a Texas Court would have no legal power to dissolve the marriage.

In general, "domiciled in Texas" means at least one spouse is a permanent resident here. For those who leave the state temporarily or who have second homes elsewhere, Texas must be the place of permanent or indefinite domicile.

Under *In Re Green,* 385 S.W.3d 665, 669 (Tex.App. -San Antonio 2012), "The test for residence or domicile typically involves an inquiry into a person's intent."

In Texas, there are two special statutes for military personnel regarding residency and domicile.

The first one is Texas Family Code Section 6.304. Under this statute, a person is not a resident of this state who is serving in the armed forces of the United States and has been stationed in the state for at least six months and at a military installation in a county of the state for at least 90 days is considered a Texas domiciliary and a resident of that county.

This is helpful for a military service member or their spouse seeking a divorce because they may not be technically a permanent resident of the state under cause law because he or she may not intend to reside here indefinitely or permanently.

The other helpful statute is Texas Family Code Section 6.303. Under this statute, if Texas was the domicile of a military member or Federal Employee when they left Texas to serve outside of Texas, that person is still able to file for divorce in Texas.

Proper Venue or Where to File

Only one party must live in the county where the divorce is filed. This means a spouse can either file in the county where they are living or the county where their spouse is living.

In either scenario, the party who is being used to meet residency requirements must have lived in that county for 90 days and have lived in Texas for six months.

Military Divorce in Texas

The term "military divorce" is used to describe a Texas divorce wherein one or both spouses is or was a member of the uniformed services. Military divorce is a descriptive term, not a legal one.

Military service member or retired military personnel have many family and property issues that are unique. These include:

1. The division of military pensions
2. Health insurance for former civilian spouses and dependents
3. Long-distance visitation during deployment
4. Devising a parenting plan
5. Managing court appearances when stationed overseas, among other important matters.

Self-Help: TexasLawHelp.org

TexasLawHelp.org is a website dedicated to providing free, reliable legal information to low-income Texans. It is part of a broader effort within the national legal aid community to use technology, specifically the Internet, to enhance and expand the delivery of legal aid.

The website provides do-it-yourself court forms for divorce and many other civil matters. Every spouse should consult with an attorney before making important decisions about child custody, property division, and financial support.

But if you would prefer to handle your divorce without legal representation, you can utilize these forms.

If you want a little more help, the Law Office of Bryan Fagan offers Texas divorce and child custody coaching. This is another do-it-yourself alternative. Every subscription includes help with Texas divorce forms and instructions, checklists, and unlimited email access to a Texas attorney.

Continuing Health Insurance Coverage Under Cobra

Texas divorce often has an impact on employer-provided group health or dental insurance coverage for dependents. Therefore, insurance availability, terms of coverage, and replacement costs should be factored into the parties' divorce just like assets and debts are.

For example, health insurance coverage should be discussed when parties negotiate spousal maintenance or a parenting plan for their children.

Unless ordered otherwise by the court or agreed by the parties as part of a spousal support package, the individual premiums on the COBRA coverage will be billed to and paid by the non-employee spouse post-divorce.

The granting of a divorce makes the non-employee spouse ineligible for group health insurance coverage that may have been available previously to all of the family members.

If a spouse's employer is subject to the federal Consolidated Omnibus Budget Reconciliation Act (COBRA) provisions (not all employers are), then after the divorce is final, health insurance coverage may be continued for dependents as qualified beneficiaries the children or a former spouse.

Both divorce and legal separation are qualifying events that trigger COBRA. As a qualified beneficiary under COBRA, the nonemployee-spouse has the right to pay the premiums and continue under his or her former spouse's employer-provided group health insurance.

While the non-employee spouse is not guaranteed the same group premium rates he or she enjoyed previously, the non-employee spouse will have uninterrupted health insurance coverage for a specified time so that he or she can obtain other coverage through that party's own employment or private carrier and can terminate the COBRA coverage.

Insurance coverage can continue under COBRA for 18 months, 29 months, even 36 months after the divorce, depending upon the facts. COBRA requires proper notice of the divorce or legal separation followed by an election period.

The employee-spouse, non-employee spouse, or qualifying dependent must notify the group health benefit plan administrator. Thereafter, the qualified beneficiary must be given an election period of at least 60 days to choose continued health care coverage under the group plan or not.

The health benefit provisions in COBRA amended the Employee Retirement Income Security Act (ERISA), the Internal Revenue Code, and the Public Health Service Act.

While state laws vary in how they address these issues, the basic principles followed by the courts when considering requests for divorce are relatively uniform.

Chapter 5

CAN I GET A LEGAL SEPARATION OR COMMON LAW DIVORCE?

Legal Separation

Some spouses may conclude that continuing to live in the marital home together is impossible, but they are unwilling or not yet ready to dissolve their marriage. Instead, they would prefer to be legally separated.

Legal separation is a concept that provides a middle ground between marriage and divorce. Some states have enacted statutes and enforce laws that allow or even require spouses to legally separate before divorcing. However, **Texas does not** recognize legal separation. In short, persons in Texas are either married or they are divorced.

Although Texas does not have a statute regarding legal separation when a couple has minor children, Texas does have a law allowing people to seek court orders regarding the children even while the couple is still married.

A parent can file a "Suit Affecting the Parent Child Relationship" (SAPCR) asking a Court to establish provisions regarding:

1. Child Support

2. Visitation

3. Rights and Duties

Unlike a divorce, the parents will not be free to marry other people and none of the couple's property or debt issues will have been resolved. If the couple decides to divorce later having done the SAPCR, it will probably not save the couple any money if they decide they need to make changes to the prior arrangement.

Common Law Divorce

A few times a year, I get a question or two regarding how to get a common-law divorce.

Brief Answer

There is no such thing in Texas as a common-law divorce. If there is a valid marriage, in order to be divorced, you must go through the same divorce process as everyone else.

1.   Common Law or Informal Marriage and Divorce

One way a divorce involving a common-law marriage can be different from a ceremonial marriage is that one of the spouses may dispute that there was ever a valid marriage. If this dispute arises, then a mini trial must commence to obtain a finding regarding the existence of a valid marriage. If the court determines that a valid marriage exists, the normal divorce process can resume.

2.   Two-Year Presumption

Some of the confusion regarding the existence of a "common law divorce" is that if a proceeding to prove informal marriage under family code is not commenced within two years after the parties have separated and stopped living together, there is a rebuttable presumption that the couple did not enter an agreement to be married. This just means the person wanting proof of a common law or informal marriage existence must put on evidence to rebut the presumption.

To prove the existence of an informal marriage, a party can present evidence of the elements of an informal marriage or by proof of either an executed declaration of informal marriage or a recorded certificate of informal marriage.

There Is No Informal Divorce

An informal marriage begins when all statutory elements are concurrently satisfied in Texas and the parties have the capacity to marry. Like ceremonial marriage, an informal marriage lasts until dissolved by death, divorce, or annulment.

Chapter 6

COMMON LAW
MARRIAGE AND TEXAS
DIVORCE

In Texas, many people are aware that Texas recognizes common-law marriage. However, not everyone that I meet with is aware of what it takes to meet the Texas statutory requirements of being common law married or why it is important.

Recently, I was meeting with a man who was bewildered that he had been sued for divorce. When I asked him about his case he plopped down an original petition for divorce and said, "I want to know how I am married?"

"Am I married?" Seems like a simple question, right? Sometimes, however, it is not.

I asked him, "You never had a ceremonial marriage?"

He answered, "No."

I then started asking him the following questions:

Q: "Have, you ever lived together?"

Answer: "Yes."

Q: "Have, you ever introduced each other as being husband and wife?"

Answer: "Yes, out of convenience."

Q: "Have, you ever filed taxes together?"

Answer: "Well we have kids together so I filed as head of household and claimed her and the kids on my tax return."

I let him know that he and his ex may be common-law married.

"Common Law marriage is something that exists in Texas, although it is called Informal Marriage under the Family Code."

Is Common-Law Marriage a Texas Thing?

In the above consult, the man was extremely frustrated that Texas had laws recognizing the Common-Law Marriage. However, Texas is not the only state with this provision. The following states have laws regarding common law marriage:

Alabama	Colorado	District of Columbia	Georgia (if created before 1/1/97)
Idaho (if created before 1/1/96)	Iowa	Kansas	Montana
New Hampshire (for inheritance purposes only)	Ohio (if created before 10/10/91)	Oklahoma (possibly only if created before 11/1/98.	Pennsylvania (if created before 1/1/05)
Rhode Island	South Carolina	Texas	Utah

The Texas Statutory Requirements for a Common-Law Marriage

An informal or common-law marriage is a marriage between two people who have not obtained a marriage license and participated in a marriage ceremony and under Texas Family Code Section 2.401:

1. Agree to be married

2. Live together in Texas as husband and wife

3. Hold themselves out to others in Texas as husband and wife

Agreement to be Married

One of the elements to establish a common-law marriage is that the parties must agree to be married.

This means that in an evidentiary hearing, the spouse alleging a common-law marriage will need to show evidence that the parties intended to have a present, immediate, and permanent marital relationship wherein they both agreed to be husband and wife.

An agreement to get married at some time in the future is not sufficient to establish an agreement to be married. If there is no written agreement to be married, your actions and the actions of the other party can be used to prove that there was an agreement to be married.

Living Together

The next element needed to establish a common-law marriage is that the parties must have lived together in Texas as husband and wife.

Texas case law states that to meet the element of living together as husband and wife, you must demonstrate that you maintained a household and did things that are commonly done by a husband and a wife.

There is no minimal number of days you must have resided together in Texas to meet this requirement.

Holding Out

The final element needed to establish a common-law marriage is that parties must have told other people in Texas that they were married.

This can be accomplished either by:

1. Spoken words, or

2. Actions and conduct by each person may be enough to fulfill the requirement of holding out.

In other words, there can be no secret common-law marriage.

Is there a Statute of Limitations on Establishing a Common-Law Marriage?

No. Contrary to what some people believe, there is not statute of limitations for establishing a common-law marriage. The following elements must be met:

1. There's an agreement to be married

2. That the couple tells other people about it

3. The couple could live together for **even one day**

This could be enough to establish a common-law marriage.

Legal Effect of a Common-Law Marriage

If a common-law marriage exists, it has the same legal significance as a ceremonial marriage. This means:

1. You would have to file for divorce when the relationship ends, just as you would if you had a ceremonial marriage.

2. Once in a common-law marriage, the only way to end it is by death, divorce, or annulment.

3. There is no such thing as a common-law divorce.

4. If a common-law marriage exists, then all property and debts accumulated during the duration of the common-law marriage are community property and are subject to division by the court at the time of the divorce.

Alternatively, a couple can file a "declaration of informal marriage" under Texas Family Code Section 2.401(a)(1) with the county clerk as prima facia evidence that the parties have entered an informal marriage.

Practically speaking, if there are children resulting from a common-law marriage or property acquired during the term of the marriage, a divorce is sometimes the best and easiest way to dissolve the relationship.

One example of this is from a case where I represented a mother, who in addition to having a child with the father, purchased a home with him. Unfortunately, when I looked at the elements to see if we could establish a common-law marriage, there was no evidence in support.

It was easy enough to establish orders regarding the child. Unfortunately, disentangling her from the house could not be accomplished at the same time and had to be pursued in a different lawsuit. This was frustrating for her because the father was living in the house rent-free and was not paying any of the bills.

Why you may want to deny the existence of a common-law marriage

The main reason people want to prove the existence of a common-law marriage is that they want to divide the property that may have been acquired during the marriage.

That is also the most common reason why someone wants to deny the existence of a common-law marriage. They want to prevent their alleged spouse from having from community property rights over any of the property.

If the party with most of the property can prevent the existence of a common-law marriage from being proven, then the alleged spouse has no rights to their property.

Proving Two People are Common-Law Married

One of the biggest differences between a common-law marriage and a ceremonial marriage is that if it is contested, the spouse alleging a marriage will need to have proof.

If the marriage is contested, it may be necessary to have a mini trial or evidentiary hearing on the existence of the marriage. If the jury or judge finds in favor of a marriage, then the divorce process will proceed as normal.

Some evidence of a common-law marriage could include:

1. Filing a federal income tax return with the other person named as your spouse;

2. Obtaining a life insurance policy and identifying the other party as your spouse and designating them as beneficiary;

3. Purchasing a home or other real property where the deed is signed by you and the other person as husband and wife;

4. Taking out a loan with the other person being identified as either your husband/wife;

5. Sending cards or letters to the other party that state "from your loving husband," or "to my loving wife;"

6. Hosting or attending an event where you introduce the other person as your spouse;

7. Your family members referring to the spouse as their son-in-law or daughter-in-law;

8. Introducing the other person to your colleagues, neighbors, and/or friends as your husband/wife.

Does Texas Recognize Common Law Marriages from Other States?

In some cases, Texas may recognize a common law marriage of a couple from another state. To prove the existence of a marriage that purportedly occurred in another state or foreign country, the party alleging a marriage will need to perform a foreign-marriage analysis.

This is done by answering a series of questions aimed at determining whether Texas Law or the law of the foreign state or country applies and whether, under that law, the requirements for proving up a marriage have been met.

These questions include:

1. Were the marriage requirements met under the laws of either state?
2. Which state's law controls?
3. Texas public policy
4. Full faith & credit clause

Public Policy

If a Texas court refuses to recognize a foreign marriage because it violates Texas public policy the parties to the foreign marriage can return to the state or country where the marriage took place and seek a divorce from there.

Full Faith & Credit

Under the full faith and credit clause, each state must give full faith and credit to the judicial proceedings, public acts, and records of other states.

Some Texas courts have held that because marriage is not a

judicial judgment and is more like a contract or license, a marriage in one state has never been considered constitutionally entitled to automatic recognition in other states.

Chapter 7

HOW LONG WILL THE TEXAS DIVORCE PROCESS TAKE?

One of the most frequently asked questions in my divorce consults is: "How soon can I be divorced?" Generally, what I tell people is that the answer depends on them and their soon to be Ex. We can get them divorced as fast as the slowest person in the relationship.

The Fast-Track Divorce

In my divorce consults, I say the divorce process starts when an Original Petition for Divorce is filed with the court. Filing the Original Petition for Divorce does two things:

1. It gives the Court Notice of what you want

2. Starts the clock on how soon you can be divorced

Under Texas Family Code Section 6.702, a "court may not grant a divorce before the 60th day after the divorce was filed." By reading this part of the family code, you learn two things:

1. The 60-day waiting period begins the day a person files for divorce

2. This means the 61st day after a divorce petition is filed is the earliest date you can get divorced in Texas.

These 60 days are often referred to as a "cooling off" period in the Texas laws. The Texas legislature decided to give the parties in a dispute, time to think through what they are doing and consider whether dissolving a marriage is a good idea.

Thus, 61 days is usually the fastest amount of time you can get a divorce in Texas. However, for the divorce to be completed that quickly, the following things will need to have been agreed on:

1. Being Divorced

2. Property and Debts

3. All Children's Issues

Divorces in Texas Often Take Longer than 61 Days

If those three things have not been agreed upon, within the 60 days, the divorce will take longer than 61 days. It is not uncommon for parties trying to work out the terms for the division of property debts, conservatorship of children, child support, and the divorce to have difficulty reaching an agreement in that short of a time.

Typically, when spouses are not able to reach an agreement, the next step is to try and get the case into mediation. At mediation, a neutral mediator will try to facilitate an agreement between the parties on all issues.

Generally, the more property and the more people whose lives are affected by the divorce, the longer the divorce will last. Again, when parties are able to agree on how to resolve these issues with each other, they speed the divorce process.

I often tell my consults it is not uncommon for a divorce in Texas to take a year. However, they can always settle the case between 61 days and one year if they reach an agreement on the three issues.

Can I get divorced sooner than 61 days?

There are exceptions to the 60-day waiting requirement under section 6.702 of the Texas Family Code. Those exceptions include:

1. A court may grant an annulment or declare a marriage void

2. The court finds that the respondent has been convicted or received deferred adjudication for an offense involving family violence as defined by section 71.004 against the petitioner or a member of the petitioner's household

3. The Petitioner has an active protective order under Title 5 or active magistrate's order for emergency protection under Article 17.292, Code of Criminal Procedure

How Soon Can I Remarry After I am Divorced?

Another common question is "how soon after the divorce can I get married?"

Under 6.801 of the Texas Family Code, a person in Texas is free to marry again 30 days after the judge signs their final divorce order, called a "decree." It is important to note that:

1. The judge does not always sign the decree on the same day that you appear in court.

2. This works in the same manner as above, meaning do not marry any one until day 31.

Exceptions to the 30-Day Waiting Period for Getting Remarried

Exceptions to this rule include:

1. Divorcing spouses under 6.801(b) may still remarry each other at any time

2. In certain cases, under section 6.802 of the Texas Family Code, a judge will waive the 30-day waiting period if good cause is shown. This requires filing a motion to request the judge to do so.

Examples of why a judge may grant a waiver of the 30-day waiting period include:

1. Health of one of the parties

2. One of the parties is scheduled to take a permanent duty reassignment in another part of the world

Chapter 8

HOW MUCH WILL MY TEXAS DIVORCE COST?

One of the most popular if not the most popular questions asked in my consults is "how much is my divorce going to cost me?" It is a reasonable question. However, there is no easy answer.

As with other professionals you hire such as a mechanic to fix your car or a plumber to fix a leaky faucet, you will get an estimate of what the service will cost. However, there are several factors that affect the cost of a divorce and many of them are beyond your control and that of your divorce lawyer. These factors make it impossible for a divorce lawyer to give you more than a guestimate of the total cost of your divorce.

Your lawyer should provide you with a quote for retaining them to represent you in your divorce. This is based on the specific circumstances of your case as discussed with your attorney.

Agreement or Trial?

There are two ways to get divorced in Texas. Either the parties will reach an agreement or the case will eventually go to trial.

The cost of a divorce in Texas depends on the ability of the parties to reach agreements. Divorce lawyers and staff members bill hourly for the time they spend on your case. I generally like to create a flow chart of typical divorce cases so people can see where in the process their money gets them.

I explain to prospective clients that many divorce cases conform to the following pattern:

1. Mediation on temporary orders
2. Temporary orders
3. Mediation on final
4. Trial

Each one of those stages may have subparts or require additional hearings in between. At each one of those stages in the divorce process, there is a chance to settle the case and not move on to the next stage. If a couple is agreeable and settles early on, then it is a lot cheaper than having to continue down the divorce path.

What I have observed is that it costs roughly $3,500-$5,500 per stage.

When I was looking for research on the cost of divorce other than my own observations, what I found was:

1. $15,00 to $20,000 – according to a July 30, 2013 article in the Huffington Post

2. $15,000 to $30,000 – according to a 2006 article on Forbes. com

3. $5,000 to $34,000 – according to a nationwide survey conducted by Nolo

These figures would be in line with my own observations of $3,500-$22,000, depending on where the parties ended up in the process.

Divorces Can Be Very Expensive

There are all kinds of jokes about divorce. One joke I like is "why does divorce cost so much?" Answer, "Because it's worth it."

In a documentary that I watched on the divorce industry, called "Divorce Corp," one of the things mentioned in the documentary was that "you can have as much justice as you can afford." What I took that to mean is that you may want to spend a lot of money on a divorce, if you can.

I have worked on multiple divorces when the legal fees on both sides were in the hundreds of thousands.

Some famous examples of expensive divorces from popular culture include:

1. Neil Diamond and Marcia Murphey at an estimated $150

million

2. Steven Spielberg's and Amy Irving's divorce at an estimated $100 million

3. Harrison Ford and Melissa Mathison at an estimated $85 million

The Total Cost of a Divorce is a Composite Number

As discussed earlier, $3,500 to $22,000 is a wide range for divorce costs with a lot of variables. This number is not just the cost of your attorney's legal fees. The ultimate number will likely be a composite of:

1. Attorney fees

2. The cost of every expert who is called to analyze your case

3. Filing fees

4. The cost of hiring a process server

5. Deposition costs

6. If bank records or other documents need to be subpoenaed

Any additional expenses related to your case will show up itemized in your bill from your attorney.

Family Law Cases are Billed by the Hour

The cost of your divorce will depend, in part, on the legal counsel you choose to represent your interests in your Texas divorce process. Attorneys bill not only for their own time, but also for the time spent by other attorneys and their staff members who work on your case.

We also have several attorneys available that we bill out at different hourly rates ranging from $175-$350 an hour. This allows us to pair your case with an attorney that can match your budget.

We also bill out our Paralegals and law clerks at rates ranging from $100-$150 an hour.

It is important to know that in most circumstances, every minute you meet with your attorney or talk on the phone is billable time. This may seem apparent, but it can be hard to remember while you are sitting in your lawyer's office enjoying a coffee or discussing your case.

Filing Fees and Costs

There are additional expenses that will need to be paid in every divorce, and these expenses are charged to you at cost. For example, the "initial filing for a divorce" is between $300-$400; this cost is passed on to you at cost.

You can usually expect to pay any filing or service fees that we must pay to the court or process server.

Additionally, you may also incur other fees such as transcript fees, expert witness fees, and mediator's fees. We generally do not charge for things like photocopies, long-distance phone calls, postage, or faxes.

Most divorce lawyers will provide you with an itemized accounting of all expenses, such as the court filing fees, deposition transcripts, and expert witness fees.

The Retainer or Prepaid Legal Fees Down Payment

A retainer is a large payment that you will pay your divorce attorney upfront. In many cases, you can think of a retainer as prepaid legal or down payment fees from which an attorney will take their hourly rate as it is earned.

As the balance of the retainer drops below a certain point, you will be asked to replenish the retainer. If your case is ongoing or proceeding to trial, your retainer may have to be replenished multiple times.

Retainers are often in the thousands or even tens of thousands of dollars. The exact cost of the retainer will depend on the complexity of your case and the level of experience your attorney possesses.

It is common to see retainers anywhere from $2,500 to $15,000 for a divorce or family law case in Texas. Complex divorce or child custody cases might require a down payment of $25,000 or more.

You will be quoted a retainer at your initial consultation and that retainer amount will be in your fee agreement. As such, any portion of your retainer that is not used should be refunded to you. It should be noted, however, that the retainer is generally not enough to cover the full cost of a divorce, and there is a good chance that you will need to replenish the retainer over the duration of your case.

Can I Make my Spouse Pay for my Attorney Fees?

In most cases, you will pay your own legal fees. Generally, unless there is a clear income disparity between you and your spouse, you each will pay your own attorney's fees and court costs. However, if there is a disparity in income, courts will sometimes "equalize" attorneys' fees at the temporary orders hearing.

Examples of a disparity of income include:

1. One party is in control of the family finances

2. One party has raided the joint bank account and left the other party with no money

Things that Can Affect the Cost of a Divorce

1. Do you have minor children?

2. Are there retirement plans between spouses?

3. Have you or your spouse committed fault?

4. Are you or your spouse financially dependent on each other?

5. Do you have a family-owned business or professional practice?

6. Are there substantial marital assets?

7. How complex is the case?

8. Are you going to trial?

Children

The most contentious cases I have seen where people fight the most usually involve children. Even if there are no other contested issues, this can greatly increase the cost of the divorce.

For example, if you and your spouse are going to both fight to be the "primary conservator," this alone can make your divorce expensive. When divorces get contentious regarding children, it is not uncommon for a judge to appoint an attorney called an Amicus to represent the children.

An Amicus attorney doesn't represent you or your spouse; they are an attorney appointed by a judge to look out for the "best interest of the children." This attorney is paid for by both you and your spouse. In one case that I worked on in which an Amicus was appointed, for our client alone, the Amicus cost was an additional $50,000. In most cases I have worked on, it has not been nearly that bad, but that does illustrate what is possible.

Going to Trial

Some of the most expensive divorces in Texas are the ones that go to trial. Part of the reason for this is because your case will have probably already been mediated multiple times, gone through the discovery process, and had a Temporary Orders Hearing. Then on top of those things, your case will likely need several additional hours preparing for a courtroom battle.

Filing for Fault in a Divorce

In Texas when divorce paperwork is filed to start the case, there is an option to file either fault or no fault.

In a no-fault divorce in Texas, the ground you cite is "insupportability," which means you no longer wish to be married to your spouse.

However, you can choose to file in Texas for one of the following fault grounds:

1. Living apart

2. Confinement in a mental hospital

3. Cruelty

4. Abandonment

5. Conviction of a felony

6. Adultery

In Texas, you can ask the court to give you the divorce because it was somebody's fault. If fault is proven, then when a court gives a divorce for "grounds," a court may give more of the community property to the "innocent" spouse.

Chapter 9

EIGHT TIPS FOR
REDUCING THE COST OF A
DIVORCE

Y ou have probably heard that divorce can be a very expensive process. This is made all the more frustrating because, at the time of divorce, you may be in the most difficult financial position you have been in.

Below are some tips to help guide you in reducing the costs of a Texas Divorce.

1. Educate yourself about Law and Assets and Debts

Learn as much as you can about Texas divorce and related issues. The more you know about the process, the less money you will spend paying a Texas divorce attorney to educate you.

Research Texas divorce laws, whether through a local law library or the internet. BryanFagan.com is a comprehensive divorce and family law website in Texas. The site features many blog articles that answers questions regarding divorce and family law.

Reading the information on this site will dramatically improve your effectiveness and efficiency in interacting with your lawyer and negotiating with your spouse.

If your spouse handles the finances, you may not know what you own and what you owe. It would therefore be a good idea to:

1. Obtain a copy of your credit report to ensure that you are aware of all open credit accounts.

2. If necessary, hire an appraiser to appraise personal and real property

3. Do some investigating to be sure that you are aware of all of your spouse's accounts.

2. Mitigate Conflict

While there has most likely been conflict in your marriage leading you to divorce, do your best to manage your emotions and not escalate the conflict in the divorce.

If you want to keep your money instead of giving it to a lawyer, go to court only as a last resort. Try negotiation, mediation, arbitration, or settlement conferences, but try not to litigate.

You may win at trial, but at what cost? Litigation is destructive, expensive, and stressful. Litigate only if you have no other option. Litigation is, unfortunately, necessary in some cases.

There are always cases and people that just cannot agree. In such cases that is why there are judges and trials.

3. Consider Mediation or Arbitration

Going to trial is expensive. While trial is sometimes necessary to resolve disputes, mediation and arbitration are alternatives to court and are almost always less costly. These processes are often quicker as well, and can be less adversarial and allow for creative solutions that are not possible at trial.

4. Try to Narrow Down Your Disagreements

By getting a list of things you and your spouse agree upon first you may be able to save money and time by only focusing on the areas of disagreement with your lawyer.

5. Control Your Emotions

In divorce, it is easy let your emotions take over and make all of your decisions. This is often a mistake, especially if you are only fighting over property.

One example of this I witnessed was when I was in mediation and almost all issues were resolved but the husband and wife were fighting over a $200 kid's bed. Both parents thought they should have it and would not budge. This argument went on for three hours. By time it was done, both parents could have bought the bed at least four times.

Lawyers can help you get past the issues on which you and your ex disagree, but if you are arguing over little things, the cost of the argument will likely be more than the cost of replacing whatever property you think you should have.

6. Don't be Penny-Wise and Pound-Foolish

Example of this can be of this could be if your lawyer advises using a particular mediator because they believe that mediator could get the case settled and you refuse because you want to use the free mediation services provided by the county.

I have seen this happen a couple times and it has not worked out for the client; the case did not settle and they ended up paying much more because the case had to go to trial.

Another example is relying on your spouse's lawyer to do all the work. An opposing counsel has no duty to you and may even have a duty to act to your detriment when it is permissible and to the benefit your spouse who hired the lawyer.

7. Take Advantage of your Divorce Lawyer's Support Staff.

You can lower your own legal fees by avoiding long telephone conversations and unnecessarily long meetings with your attorney.

When possible, speak with your attorney's legal assistants and other support staff when. They will be able to answer many of your questions as long as your question does not call for legal advice.

Legal assistants can answer questions, direct you where to go for court, look up upcoming events, and schedule you with a time to speak with your attorney. They are an important part of your representation and should be utilized whenever possible.

8. Other Ways to Lawyer your Legal Fees

You can do the "homework" your divorce lawyer gives and bring them the documents they request. By doing this, your lawyer will not have to research those things on their own and bill you for their time.

You can also take as reasonable a position as possible in negotiations in order to avoid protracted litigation.

Chapter 10

HOW WILL I PAY FOR MY TEXAS DIVORCE?

In the previous chapters, I discussed how much someone can expect to pay for their divorce and how to try and minimize those costs. However, while writing this book I had a meeting with a potential client and realized I have not discussed the topic of getting the money to pay for a divorce lawyer.

In more than one consult, I have been asked "how do I pay for your services?" My response often has been "I do not know." This is a topic I have considered at different times with no clear-cut solution. Aside from implementing payment plan options in our law firm, many of the other options depend on the circumstances of the individuals seeking our services.

Unfortunately for many people facing a divorce, one spouse is often in control of money. This can make it difficult for the spouse not in control of the finances to hire a divorce lawyer. This is because unlike other areas of the law, divorce lawyers require a large retainer before they will take your case. Texas law does not allow contingency fee divorces.

In this chapter, I will discuss various methods that I am aware that some of my clients have utilized to pay for our services when money was not readily available.

8 Ideas on How You Can Get Money to Pay for Your Divorce

1. Use your savings or rainy day fund

2. Borrow the money from friends, family, or coworkers

3. Crowdfunding your divorce

4. Apply for a credit card or personal loan

5. Borrow money from your retirement account

6. Refinance your vehicle

7. Divorce financing & payment plans

8. Selling valuable personal property

Use Your Savings or Rainy Day Fund

If you have savings, one of the things you can spend money on is a divorce lawyer. Unfortunately for many people, they do not have access to savings.

If you are not in a rush to hire a divorce lawyer, start setting up a raining day fund in case you ever need to hire a divorce lawyer.

Hopefully, you would never need to use such a fund for a divorce lawyer. However, we believe that is better to be prepared and not use such a fund than the alternative.

Borrow the Money from Friends, Family, or Coworkers

One of the most utilized methods my clients use to obtain the necessary funds to hire our services is to borrow the money from a friend, family member, or coworker.

Often it is a parent that has helped their child pay for our services. However, we have also seen siblings, other family members, or a new significant other pitch in. There have also been occasions where a coworker or boss has loaned money to one of our clients.

Crowdfunding Your Divorce

I have had more than one client utilize crowdfunding to help them pay for their divorce. It is sort of a twist on the same option as above just utilize the internet to expand the reach and ease of who you can borrow money from.

Depending on which crowdfunding site is used user can raise funds from:

1. Family

2. Friends

3. Random strangers

In order to run a successful campaign, you will need to open up about your divorce in a way that you would normally keep private. This means that friends, family members, your children, your ex, or the lawyers of your ex-spouse may have access to that information.

A judge may not look favorably upon your fundraising campaign if your children see what you're saying. You will need to be careful what you say.

Some popular crowdfunding sites include:

1. Gofundme.com

2. Kickstarter.com

3. Plumfund.com

4. Fundedjustice.com

Once you have chosen a crowdfunding platform and have your story up, you will need to let people know. This can be done by:

1. Calling

2. Email

3. Facebook or other social media

Apply for a Credit Card or Personal Loan

Taking out a loan for your divorce may be one of fastest ways to get money for the attorney retainer fee and other legal fees that will be needed.

However, there are many different types of loans to choose from. Some loans will be faster to get then others. Some places to borrow money from include:

1. Credit Cars

2. Personal Loans from a Bank or Credit Union

Borrow Money from your Retirement Account

Some of my clients have been able to borrow money from their retirement accounts to fund their divorce. However, there are some things to consider when trying to borrow money from your retirement account.

In most Texas divorce cases, the amount in a 401K plan that has been accumulated during a marriage is considered martial property. Any money borrowed may have to be accounted for during the divorce.

Some plan sponsors or employers do not require spousal consent for an employee to take a loan or make a withdrawal from his or her 401K; however, many do.

Another problem with being able to borrow retirement money is that not every 401K plan sponsor allows loans or withdrawals.

Refinance your Vehicle

Some clients have done cash-out refinance loans from their vehicle to get money to pay for their divorce.

Somethings you should consider before doing so include:

1. How much money will you be able pull out of the car?

2. What interest rate will you be offered?

3. Cars are a depreciating asset and lose value over time. This means that the loan will still be the as the car is losing value. You may be stuck in situation where you owe more than the car is worth.

Divorce Financing & Payment Plans

Some attorneys offer payment plans to pay their fees. One thing we do at the Law Office of Bryan Fagan is try and work with clients on paying their legal fees by offering payment plans.

An example of how are payment plans work be as follows:

Retainer Amount	Payment Plans for Senior Attorney	Payment Pan for Junior Attorney
$10,000	$5,000 and $1,000 a month	$2,500 and $500 a month

In this example the potential client has three options:

1. The potential client can pay the full $10,000 down and have no monthly payments

2. Alternatively, they could elect to pay $5,000 down and $1,000 a month or

3. They would work with a Junior attorney for $2,500 down and $500 a month

Selling Valuable Personal Property

It is not uncommon for valuable personal property to be sold. We have had more than one client sell their engagement and wedding rings in order to come up with money to hire us.

Before a divorce is filed, there are no orders saying what can and cannot be done with property. This means if you need to sell property so you can have access funds, you can do so. However, after paperwork is filed this may no longer be the case.

Chapter 11

DOES IT MATTER WHO FILES FIRST IN A TEXAS DIVORCE?

Many of my potential clients are concerned with filing first in their divorce case. Many of them have the impression that if they are not the first to file, they will be at a disadvantage in their case. However, that is generally not the case when both spouses are represented by divorce lawyers. As a Houston divorce lawyer, I will discuss what importance filing first has in a Texas Divorce Case.

The Petitioner in a Divorce Case

The first to file in a Texas Divorce is known as the Petitioner. Here are the ways in which being the Petitioner matter:

Choosing which County to File In

In most divorce cases, there is not an option on where to file a divorce. However, in some situations, there may be a choice. A divorce may be filed in the county where either spouse is a resident as long as residence requirements have been met. If the spouses live in different counties, there may be a choice on where to file.

In such a case, the spouses may want to rush to file for divorce first in order to ensure the courthouse in which the divorce is filed will be geographically convenient to them. I have had cases in which my clients were saved considerable time and money by filing first. This was because their ex was either having to drive four hours every time there was a court hearing or flying from out of state.

Payment of Initial Filing Fee

The spouse who files first (The Petitioner) also pays the initial filing fee. Generally, the initial filing fee is $300 to $400.

The other spouse (respondent) can file their response (an answer to the petition), which is free or maybe costing a few dollars. The responding spouse can also countersue for divorce by filing a counter-petition for divorce; this counter-petition is $50-$100. Either way, the spouse who files generally pays more in filing fees.

Setting the Tone of the Divorce

Whoever files first sets the tone of the divorce by deciding whether to plead fault or no fault in the divorce. However, this can change, because pleadings can be amended and changed by either party.

Many times, although a client has fault grounds, they want to try to pursue an amicable no-fault divorce, at least at first, and attempt to try and resolve differences in mediation. If this is not possible, the situation will be reevaluated and the pleadings will be amended to "for fault."

Going First at Trial or Other Hearings

If the divorce case ends up in a trial, the Petitioner will get to go first in the courtroom. Most divorce and family law cases do not go to trial; being the Petitioner can have an impact on trial strategy.

However, it is not uncommon for a case to have a Temporary Orders hearing and in such a hearing, the Petitioner would get to go first.

Timing and Relief Requested

'scussed above, Temporary Orders are not uncommon when a
'>s for divorce. The petitioner can request a Temporary Or-
'n the Original Petition for Divorce. The purpose of the
rders is to put in place some orders on how the parties

will behave during the divorce.

The judge is going to give orders that will remain in place during the divorce process. These orders will include guidelines regarding visitation rights with the children, conservatorship of the children, child support, who gets to remain in the marital residence while the divorce process is going on, temporary spousal support, and who will be responsible for certain bills.

By filing for divorce first, this may give you an advantage when it comes to issues at the Temporary Orders hearing. This is because you and your divorce attorney will likely have more time to prepare for this hearing than your spouse will have.

Help Prevent Assets from Being Hidden

Before a divorce is filed, there are no orders saying what you or your spouse can do. When you file first, this may also prevent your spouse from hiding assets. This is because when you file first you can ask for a Temporary Restraining Order (TRO) an order that prohibits this type of behavior.

The TRO is binding on your spouse and may help prevent against this type of underhanded behavior.

What if you are Unable to File First?

If you are unable to file first, you should not worry. As a responding spouse, you can still participate in the divorce process. You will have an opportunity to file an answer and counter-petition with the Court.

Chapter 12

STEPS FOR FILING FOR DIVORCE IN TEXAS

The next step after hiring a divorce lawyer is to initiate a divorce in Texas by filing for divorce. A Texas divorce filing often includes the following two documents:

1. An Original Petition for Divorce is always filed

2. Sometimes a Temporary Restraining Order is included

The person who files for divorce first is called the Petitioner and the person who is served with the petition is called the Respondent.

Original Petition for Divorce

The purpose of the petition is to give notice to the family court and your ex what you are asking for. This petition is a simple document that names the husband and wife and any children of the marriage and states that the petitioner is seeking a divorce and the reason for the divorce.

The petitioner must pay a filing fee to the court, usually around $300. The filing of the petition begins the mandatory 60-day waiting period before the parties may divorce.

The Original Petition for Divorce is not a court order and does not establish anything legally. It is merely a request from the petitioner to the court that they wish to have the marriage dissolved.

The petitioner may also be asking for other things from the court. The Original Petition for Divorce will generally include the following basic information:

1. Personal information about both parties: full names, the last three numbers of the Social Security Number, last three numbers of driver's license, and service address of respondent.

2. Date of marriage

3. Date of separation

4. Grounds for divorce such as "the marriage has become in-supportable because of a discord or conflict of personalities that destroys the legitimate ends of the marriage relation-ship" with "no reasonable prospect of reconciliation"

5. One or both spouses have been domiciled in Texas for at least six months and a resident of the county for the last 90 days.

6. Personal information about all minor children born to or adopted by the couple and whether they have property.

7. What kind of orders you are requesting the court to make regarding the children as to rights and duties, visitation, and child support

8. Information about whether the wife is pregnant or not

9. Information regarding assets and debts, including marital and separate property.

10. Statement of what assets should be given to which spouse (bank accounts, real property, household furnishings, retire-ment accounts, vehicles, etc.).

11. Information about the debts incurred during the marriage and which spouse should be obligated to pay each debt.

12. Request for spousal maintenance if you are seeking spousal support

13. Has a protective order been sought or is one in place?

Grounds for Divorce

A Texas divorce petition must also allege grounds or basis for the divorce. It is one of the elements of a divorce lawsuit. If you do not allege grounds, then a judge cannot grant you a divorce.

Texas is a no-fault divorce state and most Original Petition's for Divorce will simply state that the marriage has become "insupportable." In other words, the divorce is occurring because the Petitioner wants a divorce.

A divorce petition may also allege grounds for divorce such as cruelty or maybe adultery. Such acts can serve as a basis for asking the Court for a disproportionate division of property.

Divorce and Division of Property

Many people come into my office and announce to me that Texas is a "50-50" state. This is not true. Your typical divorce petition will say something like, "in a manner that the Court deems just and right, as provided by law." "Equal" is not a word that is used. In many cases, the division of community property will be divided in a 50-50 split.

However, a 60-40 split is not unheard of, depending on the circumstances. Some divorce petitions will request a disproportionate division. The petition will, consequently, go on to list various reasons for the unequal split.

Children and Requests for Conservatorship and Support

Next, the typical divorce petition will identify your children and request the court to enter orders for their conservatorship and support.

Most Original Petitions for Divorce will plead that you and your spouse should be named joint managing conservators and that either your spouse or you should be named the "primary" parent.

In some cases, it may make sense to plead for sole managing conservator. This is mostly seen in cases where there are allegations of child abuse or neglect. Often these allegations will be supported with an affidavit describing why access to the children should be restricted.

Divorce Temporary Orders

Many times, an Original Petition for Divorce will include a request for:

1. Temporary restraining order

2. Temporary orders after a hearing

A divorce in Texas cannot be finalized for at least 60 days after the date of filing and, if there are points of disagreement between you and your spouse, the process can drag on for months, even a year! Temporary orders establish a "holding pattern" while your divorce is being finalized.

Here are some things you can expect to be covered at a hearing on divorce temporary orders:

1. Exclusive possession of the family home, automobiles, and other marital property;

2. Payment of bills and living expenses;

3. Conservatorship of the children;

4. Parenting time with the children;

5. Support of the children;

6. Drug testing;

7. Psychological evaluations; and

8. Appointment of any other expert deemed necessary by the court.

If you are going to court for a temporary orders hearing, it is important to be prepared. It is not uncommon for a divorce case to drag on for several months. If that is your case, you may be living under those temporary orders a long time.

Divorce Temporary Restraining Orders and Standing Orders in Texas

As mentioned earlier sometimes, filed with the Original Petition for Divorce, is a request for the court to issue a mutual temporary restraining order (TRO), without a hearing, to facilitate maintaining the status quo until the spouses can reach an agreement or until there can be a hearing for Temporary Orders.

Generally, these requests are made in counties that do not have Standing Orders. Standing Orders are Orders that automatically go into place after a divorce or family law case is filed. Generally, they include similar provisions as temporary restraining orders.

Temporary Restraining Orders Do Not Last

In most divorce cases, a Standard Temporary Restraining Order will be granted, if it is requested by one or both spouses. There will be hearing date in which you are to appear in court. The purpose of this hearing date is to give you and your ex a chance to be heard, before the court makes an order regarding Temporary Orders that will be in place for the duration of the divorce.

Temporary Restraining Orders are good 14 days once issued by the court and then it expires by operation of law. A TRO can be extended for another 14 days if requested by one of the parties. The idea of a Temporary Restraining Order is to maintain the status quo until the Temporary Orders are in effect.

It is a Real Court Order

As mentioned earlier, the Original Petition for Divorce is not a court order but merely a request from the Court on what the Petitioner is asking for.

If the Petitioner has asked for a Temporary Restraining Order (TRO) in their petition, then a judge may grant their request if the Petitioner has also filed a proposed Temporary Restraining Order along with their request.

The rule is that for every motion or request there is an order. In this case, the Original Petition for Divorce is the motion and the Temporary Restraining Order would be the Order. Much later down the road, the Final Decree will also be the Order based on the Original Petition for Divorce.

A TRO is an order that has the full weight and authority of the divorce court behind it. If a party to the divorce violates a TRO, the court can hold that person in contempt of court. That may mean a fine, having the pleading struck, and possible jail time.

One of the unique things regarding Temporary Restraining Orders is that they are issued *ex parte* or without prior notice to you. Also, divorce courts require no proof to issue such orders and, provided it is in proper form, a temporary restraining order will be issued automatically by the divorce court, no questions asked.

Temporary Restraining Orders are Not Protective Orders

Some questions I get asked regarding a TRO include:

1. Can I sleep at home tonight?

2. Can I talk to my spouse?

3. Can I use my credit card?

4. Can I see my kids?

5. Can my kids stay with me?

6. Can I hire a lawyer?

A Texas Divorce Temporary Restraining Order is not a protective order; this is a common misconception. Generally, this temporary restraining order has more to do with maintaining the status quo and in most cases not to keep an individual from being around another individual or location.

A Texas Divorce Temporary Restraining Order is serious; you should review the order with a divorce attorney to help you understand exactly what you can and cannot do once you have been served with a restraining order.

What Does a TRO Do?

A typical Texas Divorce Temporary Restraining Order general restricts:

1. Conduct regarding your children

2. Conduct regarding property

3. Altering or disposing of documents

Your conduct towards your spouse and your kids:

1. Do not use foul language when talking with your spouse; do not harass her with e-mails, phone calls, or text messages.

2. Do not threaten him with bodily harm.

3. Do not threaten your spouse with doing something that is just stupid.

4. Do not withdraw your kids from school or daycare.

5. Do not hide your kids from your spouse.

6. Do not move off with your children.

7. Do not say bad things to your children about the other parent.

Your conduct towards your property:

1. Do not sell any marital property.

2. Do not alter any important documents.

3. Do not give away property to your mother.

4. Do not cash out your retirement, money market, or stock accounts.

5. Do not cancel your spouse from health insurance coverage.

6. Do not spend money on anything other than necessities or normal items.

Your duty to preserve documents:

1. Do not alter or dispose of financial records.

2. Do not intercept mail that is not yours.

3. Do not wipe your computer hard drive clean.

Temporary Restraining Orders Allow

Even with a TRO in place:

1. You may talk to your spouse in a civil and constructive manner.

2. You may spend time with your children and even keep them in your care.

3. You are allowed to spend money related to your business, your living expenses, and your attorneys' fees.

4. You may hire a divorce attorney.

Chapter 13

SERVICE OF PROCESS

It is required under the Texas Family Code that a spouse be notified when a divorce case has been opened. This means they must be informed that you, the Petitioner, have asked the court to do something that might affect the Respondent's legal rights. It is not enough for you the Petitioner to tell the Respondent about the lawsuit. You must follow the Texas Rules of Civil Procedure in giving legal notice.

Methods of Service

There are four methods approved under the Texas Rules of civil procedure for giving legal notice or delivering divorce papers; those include personal service, service by certified mail, substituted service, and publication.

Personal service is the best choice for service and the one we are going to focus on in this article. This means the process server will hand deliver the divorce petition to your spouse. By using this method, the court knows that your spouse has received notice of the divorce and when personal service is accomplished.

When the divorce paperwork is filed, you will be required to fill out a service request in order to have the legal notice and divorce papers delivered to your spouse. You can select to have papers delivered by a constable or sheriff or private process server. If you want the county to handle it, you will pay for the constable to deliver the papers. If you want to use a private process server, you will fill out the contact information for the private process server you want to use and the district clerk will call the private process server to come pick up the divorce papers when they are ready for delivery.

1.   Constable / Sheriff

A constable usually costs a little less and if your spouse lives in the county, this may be a good route to take. However, if they do not live in the county, you may have to pay an additional fee and have the paperwork shipped out of county to a constable who is local to your spouse.

2.   Private Process Server

Alternatively, you can hire a private process server who works in more than one area. This is often a quicker route to take than paying for a constable to deliver the divorce paperwork. There are networks of private process servers, meaning if the server you hire does not service an area, such as when your spouse is out of state, they can get in contact with a process server in that area to get the spouse served.

3.   Waiver of Service

Another under option is available under the Texas Family Code if the respondent is willing to sign a Waiver of Service. A waiver of service is a document the Respondent spouse signs waiving the requirement for service. By signing the waiver of services, the spouse agrees that it is not necessary to have them served by a process server for the divorce case.

Chapter 14

WHAT DOES DEFAULT JUDGMENT MEAN IN A TEXAS DIVORCE?

M any times, the reason people end up in my office is because they are concerned because their spouse has sued them for divorce and the paperwork is talking about a default judgment. They ask what is a "default divorce?"

Personal Service is Required in a Texas Divorce

As we discussed in the prior chapter, every person in Texas involved in a lawsuit including a divorce is entitled to personal service of a copy of the lawsuit that was filed with the court.

When I am being asked about a "default judgment," it is because the person asking has experienced "personal service" when a constable or a private process server has handed them a copy of the original petition for divorce and a citation.

Under Texas Rules of Civil Procedure 99, the citation states that the respondent who was served with the divorce will provide the following notice:

"You have been sued. You may employ an attorney. If you or your attorney do not file a written answer with the clerk who issued this citation by 10:00 a.m. on the Monday next following the expiration of twenty days after you were served this citation and petition, a default judgment may be taken against you."

What is a Default Judgment?

A default judgment in a divorce is when the person who was served with the divorce petition fails to file a written answer as they were directed to in the notice within the required time.

This failure to respond allows the person who filed for divorce to seek a default judgment from the court. A default judgment is a judgment entered by the divorce court. This judgment will basically be for whatever is asked for by the person who filed for divorce within reason.

The asking party will still have to provide evidence show:

1. The property division is "just and right"
2. What they are asking for in regards to the children is in their "best interest"

However, I always tell people it is easy to win a one-sided argument. If the other spouse is not there to contradict them then the court only has one set of facts to go on.

A written answer is a document filed with the court stating you are aware that you have been sued for a divorce and you are answering the divorce lawsuit. If you do as you are instructed, then your spouse will not be able to get default divorce and the divorce process will continue as usual.

What is the Time Period to Obtain a Default Judgment?

In the notice, the time period given was "the Monday next after the expiration of 20 days." However, there is another important date in a divorce. That date is the day the Original Petition for Divorce was filed.

That is because a divorce in Texas has a mandatory 60-day waiting period before you can finalize the divorce. This means that day 61 from when the Original Petition for Divorce has been filed is the soonest a divorce can be finalized. So, it is important to pay attention to both of these dates when calculating when your answer is due.

To calculate the answer period, find the day the Respondent was served on a calendar, count out 20 more days (including weekends), then go to the next Monday. This is the last day of the Respondent's answer period.

You may have a little bit more protection if the 60-day waiting period is not up. However, for other reasons you still want to get your answer filed prior to the "Monday next after the expiration of 20 days."

Requirements for Obtaining a Default Divorce

If a spouse being served with divorce paperwork:

1. Has been personally served with the divorce petition

2. Has not answered the lawsuit in the stated time period

3. The citation of application and affidavit of default, has been returned to court and has been on file for at least 10 days

The petitioner in the divorce may then obtain a default divorce.

What's next?

It's important that a court reporter make a record of what is said at a default hearing. Ask the clerk if a court reporter will be available. It's a good idea to have all of your paperwork reviewed by a lawyer before going to court. You can hire a lawyer just to review your paperwork.

Evidence in Court

When requesting a default divorce from a Family Law Court, the requesting spouse will be required to have the following documents:

1. Final Decree of Divorce

2. BVS

3. Wage Withholding Order (if there are children)

4. Medical Support Order (if there are children)

5. Child Support Information Sheet (if there are children)

6. TFC Section 105.006 (if there are children)

7. Court Report Information Form

8. Certificate of Last Known Address

9. Service Member Civil Relief Act Affidavit

You will also need to be prepared to present evidence for each thing you are requesting in your Final Divorce Decree.

For example, if you are requesting something other than a Standard Possession Order in regards to visitation for the other parent, you must prove to the judge why the schedule you are presenting is in the "best interest of the children."

If you are asking for child support, you must provide information about the other parent's income. If you don't know the other parent's income, you may be able to ask the judge to base child support on the minimum wage.

The judge will go over the documents you have filed to make sure you can finish your case by default.

The judge will ask you to testify to "prove-up" your case. If at the end of the hearing, you have prepared all the necessary forms and put on all the required evidence, the judge should grant the divorce.

Chapter 15

HOW TO DRAFT AND FILE AN ANSWER TO A TEXAS DIVORCE

Once the initial shock and panic of being sued by your spouse for divorce wears off you probably have thought to yourself, "now what in the world do I do?" Well, as I have mentioned in prior articles, you must act. Doing nothing will result in your ex being able to default you for divorce. Your first step is to put together a response to their Original Petition for Divorce.

What do the Divorce Documents that I have been Served with Mean?

Before we get into the nitty gritty of how you actually draft your answer it is helpful to go over what various documents contain and what they are called. At this stage, you likely have at least two documents:

1. The Original Petition for Divorce

2. The Citation

Answer

The formal document you draft in response to the Original Petition for Divorce is called an "Answer." This is the document we are going to learn how to draft and file in this article.

At its most basic, an "Answer," is a response you file with the court letting the court know that you are planning to participate in the divorce process and do not want the court to grant a default judgment.

The other thing the Answer does is require that if any additional actions are taken in the case like a hearing, or if an order is presented to the court, you will be entitled to receive a notice of that hearing date or that document that has been filed with the Court.

In Texas, your answer should include a "general denial." Many people I meet get confused about what a "general denial" means. All a general denial means is that you want your spouse to give evidence of the things that they are saying in their divorce petition. You are not saying the things in the divorce petition are untrue.

Why you Need to File an Answer in a Divorce

Something that you may not realize is that a Divorce is a lawsuit. There are two to three things that the divorce lawsuit deals with. First, once the divorce is granted you will be divorced. Second, it will divide up property and debts. Finally, it will make provisions regarding any children of the marriage.

Once you are served with the lawsuit (the divorce papers), you will have very little time to respond. In Texas divorce papers, there will be a long paper saying you have been sued and you have until the Monday next following 20 days after service of the lawsuit to respond.

It is very important to respond by filing an answer; this prevents your spouse from being able to obtain a default judgment.

A default judgment would be judgment in favor of your spouse based on your failure to take action. It basically amounts to a one-sided argument made in front of a judge. This means the judge will only hear your spouse's side of the divorce case and rules based on the evidence that your spouse provides to the judge.

Another possible scenario is that your spouse may ask you to sign a waiver of service. Never sign one of these!

What does an Answer Look Like?

The following forms are available for download from www.bry-anfagan.com:

1. Answer for a divorce with no children

2. Answer for a divorce with children

Answer to a Divorce with No Children

Section 1 – This is a General Denial as explained above; it just means you are asking that your spouse put on evidence of the things they are saying in the original petition for divorce.

Section 2 – Is your contact information. You need to fill this section out so you can receive notices from the court of any hearing dates.

Section 3 – Separate property. If you owned anything prior to marriage, inherited, or received gifts, you should fill this section out.

Section 4 – If you want to change your name back to a name you used prior to marriage you should fill this section out. It is a lot simpler and cheaper to restore your name during a divorce than it would be after a divorce.

Section 5 – Request for Judgment. This is just your request to the court to give you the things you asked for above.

Section 6 – Certificate of Service. This is just you promising to give a copy of the Answer to either your spouse or their attorney.

Answer to a Divorce with Children

This answer is the same as above except the style of the case is different and has a place to fill out your children's names.

The Answer is Drafted—Now What?

Now that you have drafted the Answer, it is time to get it filed with the district clerk where the divorce case has been filed. Print out the original, sign it, and then make two copies.

Go down to the courthouse and file the document with the clerk. Ask the clerk to stamp the other two copies you brought with you.

Keep one copy for your records and mail a copy of your Answer to your ex or their attorney if they are represented. Most courts will not send your spouse a copy of your Answer. So it is important you do this so they know not to proceed with the paperwork for a default judgment.

Harris County, Texas

If your divorce was filed in Harris County, Texas, then you will need to file it at 201 Caroline, 2nd Floor, Room 210. Houston, TX 77002. Monday - Friday, 8:00 a.m. - 4:30 p.m.

Montgomery County, Texas

If your divorce was filed in Montgomery County, Texas, then you will need to file it at 301 N Main St, Conroe, TX 77301. Monday – Friday, 8:00 a.m. – 5:00 p.m.

Chapter 16

PREPARING YOUR DIVORCE CASE FOR MEDIATION

It is not uncommon for some of the people who consult with me regarding a divorce to ask why they need to go to mediation. Is mediation required to get a Texas divorce? The answer is no, mediation is not mandatory to divorce in Texas.

I have found, though, in most cases, mediation is a very good way to settle divorce cases in a manner that allows for certainty of the outcome and a way to control cost.

Why Mediation?

In Harris County and Montgomery County, mediation has become almost universally accepted and may be required in family law cases. When the petitioner and respondent each have a family law attorney from one of the above counties, they rarely question why we do it. However, for an individual who does not practice family and divorce law and for whom this is their first experience with a lawsuit, the why is not quite so clear.

As I mentioned earlier, mediation is not required to settle a divorce case when the parties are agreed. However, many courts in Harris and Montgomery counties require the parties to attempt mediation before asking for a hearing on:

1. Temporary Orders

2. Final Trial

This means that if you need a hearing, mediations may not only be a requirement, but a stepping-stone before you can progress to the next step in your divorce. I sometimes get the question, "can we ask the court to waive the mediation requirement because I know we will never settle?"

Yes, we can ask the court to waive the mediation requirement. However, that involves filing a motion and setting that motion for a hearing. Unless there is a good reason, like family violence, there is a good chance the judge will say no. This means in most cases it is probably easier and cheaper just to check the box and go to mediation.

If you think of mediation as a stepping-stone, you may be tempted to prepare for the mediation in a casual manner. However, a better way to prepare for mediation even if the mediation may be unsuccessful is as if you are getting ready for trial. This is because if you settle in mediation then the case is done and costs are minimized. If you do not settle, then you are ready for a court hearing.

Benefits to mediation, other than "the judge made us do it" include:

1. Creativity

2. Cost savings

3. Relationship savings

4. Privacy and confidentiality

5. Lawyers to be an advocate

6. Successful resolution

Mediation Allows Creativity

One benefit of mediation is that it allows for greater creativity and customization than going to court. In court, a judge is limited to what is in the Texas Family Code in deciding the outcome of a case. Parties often want a judge to give them a customized and creative solution to their problems. Unfortunately, because of time and the tools available to a judge in the Texas Family Code, this is just not possible.

However, through mediation, the possibilities available to parties are much greater because "tools" are much more exhaustive and are for the most part only limited by imagination and what can be agreed upon. Parties can agree to almost anything that is not illegal. Texas case law also says that judges are extremely limited in their ability to refuse to enter a decree based on the agreement of the parties in a mediated settlement agreement.

This means that things would be harder to get a judge to order such as:

1. 50/50 time with the children

2. No child support

3. Split custody

4. Paying certain bills as child support

These subjects and more are possible through mediation, whereas they would be very unlikely if the case were in front of a judge.

Mediation Allows Cost Savings

One of the most frequently cited reasons for attending mediation is that it can save you a lot of money, versus going to trial. This is likely true, and has been my experience in most cases. However, mediation does not necessarily save money in all cases. If, as my clients some-times tell me, "this case will never settle," turns out to be true, it may be an additional expense.

However, even when that turns out to be the case I do not believe me-diation is a waste of money and effort. I would say over 90% of the time, I learn more about a case from mediation than I did before. This is generally because I only have my client's perspective about a case, and during mediation I get to learn more about the facts the other side deems important, which allows me to better prepare for the trial case.

One way to maximize the chances of settling the case in mediation and reducing the cost of divorce is by being careful not to cut corners going into the mediation. This means preparing for the mediation and having:

1. Financials ready

2. Inventory and appraisement done

3. Proposed property division

4. Proposed visitation order, etc.

Mediation Allows Relationship Savings

Another reason often given for mediating a case versus going to court is that it can help save the relationship. The idea behind this is if the case goes into a public courtroom, often the parties will be saying hurtful, embarrassing, and possibly untrue things about the other party. This behavior can damage or worsen the party's relationship.

Something the parties should consider is that they will be co-parenting their children for nearly two decades after their divorce. If the case goes to trial, you can expect to spend tens of thousands of dollars on the trial. Generally, afterwards one of the parties will be unhappy and you can expect that they will be looking for a chance to take the case back to trial. One philosophy is that discussing compromising information and reaching agreements out of court in mediation can be a much better way to handle disputes.

Mediation Allows Privacy and Confidentiality

The mediation process receives strong privacy protection under Texas law. Generally, one way to look at it is that what is discussed in mediation stays in mediation. Mediation takes place outside of court, often in a private office, and this means you do not have the general public listening to your case as you would in a courtroom. The parties, lawyers, and mediator are not allowed to discuss what happens in mediation in the courtroom. This privacy allows parties to have an open discussion and make offers to settle the case without the fear of what they are saying being used against them in court. There are very few exceptions to the privacy rule. The main exceptions are regarding:

1. Child abuse or neglect

2. Elder abuse or neglect

Mediation Allows Lawyers to be Advocates

A lawyer can advocate for their client at mediation to a degree. It is important to realize the mediator does not make decisions about the case. The mediator's job is to settle the case. A settled case can take a lot of different forms.

A lawyer can discuss a client's options and why an offer is a good deal or the client could do better in trial. Additionally, an attorney can spin certain facts and give a mediator information that the mediator can use as leverage to move the opposing side in the other room.

Mediation Allows Successful Resolution

Statistically, family law and divorce parties who go to mediation resolve their differences in mediation more often than they do not. Depending on the source, you will hear that 80% to 95% of family law cases settle in mediation. The successful resolution of divorce and family law cases is one of the main reasons judge's order parties to attend mediation before coming to trial.

Another good reason is that if the case settles, it is done; you and your spouse do not get to change your mind about the agreement the next day. You are both stuck with the agreement unless you can both agree to change something. This also relates back to cost savings that were discussed above. If the case is over, then you do not need to keep spending money fighting.

Unfortunately, not everyone prepares as thoroughly for mediation as they should to take advantage of all the benefits of mediation.

5 Things to Do to Prepare for Mediation

Preparing your case for mediation is as important as preparing your case for trial. As part of your preparations, it is important to:

1. Exchange inventories and appraisements and supporting

documents (and do discovery when necessary);

2. Exchange settlement offers and reach agreements;

3. Prepare a spreadsheet of assets and liabilities if property is at issue;

4. Send the mediator a confidential position statement and a copy of pleadings, sworn inventories, supporting documents, a property spreadsheet, a summary history of the case, and the client's goals; and

5. Talk to the mediator.

Exchange Inventories, Appraisements, and Supporting Documents

Before coming to mediation, I like to insist that parties exchange their sworn Inventory and Appraisements. It is not uncommon for me to sometimes encounter some initial resistance from my client on preparing an inventory. One of the excuses I hear is that "we do not share any property; it's all in my name/her name."

I then must explain how community property works; it doesn't matter whose name is on any property. I explain the easiest and cheapest way to settle the case is if we know what property and debts exist. If we do not have the information prior to mediation, we can settle the case on temporary but we will not be able to settle the case on final basis.

At the very least you should include:

1. The latest statement on all asset and liability accounts

2. Any supporting documentation for the parties claimed value on real property and other assets of value.

If the opposing party will not agree to exchange inventories, or if you still have financial questions after exchanging inventories, then it may be necessary to conduct discovery to help fill in some of the financial gaps.

Exchange Settlement Offers and Reach Agreements

It may seem strange to talk about exchanging settlement offers and reaching agreements before coming to mediation. Offers can be exchanged prior to mediation:

1. If there is a good relationship still between a husband and wife, they may be able to reach an initial settlement agreement. This can turn a four-hour mediation into one-hour mediation where the initial agreement is just polished and finalized.

2. The issues can be narrowed for the actual mediation allowing the parties, the mediator, and their attorneys to focus on the issues that are really disputed or that are most important to the parties.

3. The mediator will have a head start by being able to review those offers prior to mediation.

4. A mediator will know which issues have potential for an early agreement and those that will need more negotiation.

It is not uncommon in mediation for parties to reach what is known as a partial Mediated Settlement Agreement. When this happens, the remaining issue or issues are taken in front of a judge to be resolved. This means instead of having to have a full hearing the parties will have a shortened hearing. This means the hearing in front of the judge should be less expensive because the parties can focus on only the disputed issues.

Exchanging offers prior to mediation serves the same purpose as reaching a partial mediated settlement agreement in mediation. If agreements can be reached on the easy issues, then the mediator can focus on only the disputed issues saving time and money.

This is something you will want to discuss with your attorney because although something might not be important to you, it may be very important to the other party. Sometimes mediation is like a game of chess where you may be willing to exchange a piece, but you want to get a higher-value piece for that exchange. An example might be:

1. Your spouse wants to move back home and not be bound by a geographical restriction. This is something you would be more than happy to agree to.

2. You would like a reduction in your child support.

If you take the geographical restriction off the table because you do not care about it, there may be no incentive for your ex to agree to no geographical restriction.

Prepare a Proposed Property Division or spreadsheet of Assets and Liabilities

A Proposed Property Division or spreadsheet of assets and liabilities is a helpful tool for parties, lawyers, and the mediator to use while mediation is ongoing. It can also speed the preparation of the mediated settlement agreement.

Generally, my office will take a laptop and printer to mediation so that as negotiations progress, we can update printout updated versions of this document throughout the mediation, often the final version is then attached to the mediated settlement agreement as an exhibit.

We will often email this spreadsheet to the opposing side before or during mediation so that we are using the same spreadsheet at mediation.

This helps make a complicated property case easier. It can get very convoluted if the parties and their attorneys are using different spreadsheets where everything is arranged differently or does not include all the same property.

Prepare a Mediation Letter for the Mediator

We like to communicate with the mediator prior to mediation. One way is by putting together a mediation package that we forward to the mediator. Usually included in this package is:

1. A letter from us regarding what has happened so far in the case and what some of the important issues may be.

2. A letter from our client providing some background information on the parties, what they think should be important for the mediator to know, and what they want.

3. Copy of pleadings

4. Sworn inventories

5. Supporting documents

6. A property spreadsheet

Most mediators, if we get this information to them far enough in advance, will review materials prior to the mediation. By taking the time to send the mediator this information in advance allows:

1. The mediator to get a head start on what the issues are in the case.

2. The mediator to study the case and develop an understanding of the parties, their children, and the property.

Talk to the Mediator Prior to Mediation

It is sometimes helpful to talk with the mediator prior to the actual mediation. Sometimes this takes the form of:

1. A phone call a day or two in advance of the mediation

2. Just meeting with the mediator at mediation before the mediation starts

The phone call is often helpful in cases where there are already some agreements; it can help iron out a lot of the details prior to the parties arriving so that there is already a draft mediated settlement agreement ready.

It is quite common for the attorneys and mediator to meet prior to the start of mediation. Many mediators use this as an opportunity to ascertain what specific issues or concerns need to be addressed by the mediator to begin with.

Attorneys can also use this meeting as an opportunity to:

1. Alert the mediator to things that are important to their client. Sometimes this meeting is with both attorneys at the same time or with the attorneys separately.

2. Clarify the case to the mediator when the case has unusual facts, multiples parties, or an unusual client.

Chapter 17

THE DIVORCE
TEMPORARY ORDERS

What occurs between filing and finalizing a divorce case in Texas?

One of the biggest concerns spouses have after filing for divorce is, "What happens now?" It is vital for you to fully understand all the stages of the divorce process so that there will not be surprises during the pendency of your case. Knowledge and preparation are key to positive outcomes for you and your family.

Divorce Temporary Orders

Once the divorce is filed, it is time to take stock of your situation. Things to consider include:

1. How community expenses are going to paid

2. Who will have use of and possession of specific community property such as vehicles and the marital residence

3. Who will be the primary parent in possession of the children

4. What sort of visitation the children will have with the parents

5. The amount of temporary child support

6. Which parent will be responsible for providing health insurance

7. Temporary spousal support

8. Whether one spouse will pay for the interim attorney fees for the other spouse, and

9. Whether temporary injunctions be put in place

It may be necessary if the parties cannot agree on the above issue to ask the court for orders to determine how the parties' relationship with the children and finances will be handled while the divorce is ongoing. These court orders are called "temporary orders" and can include temporary provisions ordering:

1. The payment of temporary alimony

2. The payment of temporary child support

3. Temporary residency restriction for the children

4. Temporary conservatorship/custody of the children

5. Temporary medical support

6. Temporary possession of and access to the children (possession schedule)

7. Which spouse pays specific debts during the divorce process

8. Temporary exclusive use of motor vehicles

9. Temporary payment of expenses related to the household, including mortgage and utilities

10. Temporary payment of insurance premiums, including auto insurance, health insurance, life insurance, and homeowner's insurance

11. Temporary exclusive use of personal property and furnishings

12. Payment of attorney fees

13. Temporary exclusive use of the marital residence

14. Who has the use of other community property, such as vehicles

Maintaining the Status Quo

Often the court does not want to make any major changes to the lives of the parties by its orders. This might mean that the court will prevent a party from substantially changing accounts and policies in order that the community estate and the parties are protected financially.

An example of this would be the court ordering a party to maintain health insurance on his or her spouse and the children. Another example of maintaining the status quo would be the court ordering that the parties have the exclusive use of the vehicle that they normally drive. This does not mean they will get that vehicle on final orders

Are Temporary Orders Required?

Temporary Orders are not mandatory. Some spouses can work together informally to take care of issues related to property, bills, and children, child support, payment of debts, and possible temporary spousal support.

Is a Court Hearing Required to Obtain Temporary Orders?

It is not always necessary to go to court to obtain Temporary Orders; sometimes it is possible to negotiate formal Temporary Orders outside of court. Sometimes this is done over the phone and then orders are drafted. Sometimes this is done through mediation prior to a Temporary Orders Hearing.

When Negotiations Fail

If Temporary Orders cannot be worked out informally and a dispute arises, a party can request a hearing before a judge to obtain temporary orders. These Temporary Orders will remain in place until the final divorce decree is entered or the court makes additional orders.

A temporary orders hearing is often like a mini-trial or a preview of what the final trial will look like. The attorneys present arguments, examine witnesses, and present evidence before the judge. This gives the judge an idea of the temporary issues at hand that need to be decided.

These orders are temporary and generally designed to maintain the parties' status quo until the case is finalized. However, tactical advantages can be gained during this stage with respect to final child custody or property division. You can also see in what direction a judge is leaning on the particular issues in the case.

Chapter 18

GETTING READY FOR A TEMPORARY ORDERS HEARING

Often it feels that the Temporary Orders hearing comes very quickly. There have been times when I have received only three days' notice to prepare. This chapter is designed to answer common questions that many people have regarding temporary orders hearing and gives you an idea of what to expect when preparing for the hearing and when you testify. The ideas in this article will apply not only to clients, but in part also to other witnesses.

Steps and Exhibits for Aid in a Temporary Orders Hearing:

1. Write a history of your marital relationship with your spouse. This history should contain dates and facts supporting your claim for custody.

2. Make a list of all the reasons why you are best for custody, with supporting facts and dates.

3. Make a list of all the reasons why your spouse should not be appointed custodian of the child, with supporting facts and dates.

4. Make a list of all witnesses you will need at the temporary hearing, names, addresses, telephone numbers, and a summary of what they know. Also, determine if they need a subpoena.

5. Fill out the financial information statement on your income and living expenses.

6. Make an appointment with your attorney to discuss strategy, if possible seven days prior to the hearing date.

7. Develop a plan to manage the child now—from day to day, while you are employed.

Necessary Financial Information for a Temporary Orders Hearing

During a Temporary Orders hearing, it is important to bring certain financial documents to show the court, so that the judge can use that information to help make financial orders that will last during the pendency of the divorce.

Typically, the documents needed include:

1. Your three most recent pay stubs

2. Your prior year's tax return

3. W-2s from the prior tax year

4. Any 1099s

5. All documents pertaining to any life, casualty, liability, and health insurance

6. Documentation as to the cost the family's health insurance as well as documentation as to the cost of only the children's monthly health insurance amount.

Failure to provide these necessary documents can have a negative impact on you during the pendency of the divorce.

Negative Facts

You **do not** want your divorce lawyer to find out negative facts for the first time at the Temporary Orders Hearing. By discussing negative information prior to the hearing, your lawyer can prepare for these facts such as:

1. Your past criminal history

2. Drug use

3. Your new boyfriend or girlfriend that your ex does not ap-

prove of

4. CPS history

5. Any other "skeletons in your closet"

Discussing these issues with your divorce lawyer before hearing may help your attorney to try to minimize the impact of these "skeletons" on your case.

Witnesses

If there are witnesses who would be helpful to your case, you will need to provide your attorney with their name and contact information as early as possible. This will allow your lawyer enough time to issue any necessary subpoenas to secure the attendance of witnesses for your hearing.

You should let your witnesses know that your lawyer will be contacting them about their possible testimony in your case.

Determining Temporary Custody of the Children

There are several factors a judge considers when deciding who should be given the temporary exclusive right to establish the primary residence of the child.

If both parents are fit and there has not been any child abuse, harm, or neglect, a judge is going to be looking to see which parent has been the primary caretaker of the child. Some things a judge considers when making this determination include:

1. Who feeds your child

2. Who bathes your child

3. Who gets the child ready for school

4. Who takes the child to school or daycare

5. Who picks up your child from school or daycare

6. Who takes the child to and from doctors' appointments

7. Who attends school activities and parent-teacher conferences

8. Who participated in the child's extracurricular activities

9. Who helps with the child's homework

Visitation During Temporary Orders

If parents can agree, they can establish any visitation schedule they want that fits their needs and those of the children.

If the parents are unable to agree to a possession schedule, the presumption in Texas is that a court should order what is called the "standard possession order." In Texas, the standard possession schedule is based on a suggested order in the Family Code. There is a presumption that a standard possession schedule in all cases involving a child over the age of three is in the "best interest of the child."

If the divorcing parties live within 100 miles of each other, the standard possession schedule provides for possession by the parent with whom the children do not primarily reside as follows:

1. Beginning at 6:00 p.m. or when school is dismissed on the first, third, and fifth weekends of each month and

2. Ending at 6:00 p.m. on the following Sunday or when school resumes the following Monday;

3. Every Thursdays during the school year each week from 6:00 p.m. to 8:00 p.m. (or from the time school lets out until the time school resumes on the following day);

4. Alternating Thanksgiving and spring break holidays, even number for Thanksgiving and odd number for spring break and reversing the following year; part of the Christmas break.

What to Wear

In most cases, a Temporary Order hearing will be the first time the judge in your case will have a chance to observe you. The judge will be deciding issues regarding you, your spouse, and your children. It is important to present yourself in a good light.

If you will be testifying, you need to dress for your testimony as if you were going to church. Women need to wear darker clothing, no expensive flashy jewelry, and light makeup. Men should wear a suit, or at least a tie.

Everyone is nervous before testifying. Never, however, "fortify" yourself for testimony by taking tranquilizers, drinking alcohol, or having anything else that will either slow down or speed up your nervous system.

If you are testifying, remember that you will be observed both in and out of the courtroom by jurors (perhaps), attorneys, witnesses for the other side, and sometimes, the judge. Jurors, if any, may see you in the elevator or on the stairway at the courthouse, or in the restroom or on the street. They may see you driving to the courthouse in your car.

It is important that you conduct yourself in a courteous manner at all times. Obviously, a witness is not going to make a good impression on the stand if he has had an unfriendly encounter with a juror in traffic, or, if after his testimony, a juror hears him in the hall laughing at something humorous that occurred in the courtroom. While you are at the courthouse, either before or after your testimony, be serious, do not joke with other witnesses or attorneys, or do anything else that might give a juror the impression that you are taking your testimony, or the case itself, lightly.

If your case is to a jury, try to avoid the individual jurors. A friendly smile to a juror is all right if it is not forced. You might even say "good morning." But under no circumstances should you ever enter into any conversation with any juror for any reason at any time. The same rules will apply to the judge.

Below are some suggestions for preparing yourself for court:

1. Make sure your hair is clean and combed

2. Your facial hair should be groomed, neat, and clean

3. Wear slacks and a shirt with a collar if you own them

4. Do not wear a tank top or sleeveless shirt

5. Do not wear shorts

6. If you wear a skirt, make sure that it is not too short

7. Do not wear clothing that exposes your underwear

8. Do not wear flip-flops

9. All shirts need to cover your stomach

10. Do not show too much skin in court

11. Do not wear a hat or cap to court

12. Do not chew gum in the courtroom

13. Turn off your cell phone prior to entering the courtroom

Testimony in Court

You are about to testify in a Temporary Orders hearing. Testimony takes place in the courtroom before a judge. You will be testifying at a temporary hearing. Testimony in a final hearing may be to a judge or, in some cases, to a jury.

At either the temporary hearing, or the final hearing, there may be a court reporter present, a bailiff, both parties, and their attorneys.

Tell the Truth

Always tell the truth when testifying. Failure to tell the truth constitutes perjury, a crime under the Texas Penal Code. Tell the truth to the best of your ability, whether it may "help" our side's case, or "hurt" our case. Do not exaggerate or try to make anything seem better or worse than it really is.

I hope that you have not held anything back in our previous conversations. Some clients and witnesses feel that, if they do not tell everything to their lawyer, the other side may not know or be able to find out about the concealed facts. The problem with this approach is that the other side may know those detrimental facts, or learn about them, while I am not aware of them. The only way that I can be properly prepared to explain or perhaps overcome the impact of detrimental facts is to know about them in advance, and not hear about them for the first time at a hearing or trial.

The corollary to this rule is that, once I am aware of these facts, I cannot allow you, if asked a question about these detrimental facts, to be untruthful about them.

It is also important for me to know if you have ever had any prior arrests, criminal convictions, or other allegations of wrongdoing to misdeeds made against you, whether fairly or not. It is possible that the other side may try to use this to "impeach" your testimony, and therefore, it is important for me to be aware of this information.

Finally, if you have made any statements to police officers, investigators, etc., whether orally or in writing, you need to let me know about that. You have a right to copies of any written statements which you have made. Additionally, if you have written any letters, cards, or other writings to the other side, which bear on any issues in the case, you need to let me know. This is particularly true if those writings contain information you might not want to hear in the courtroom. The same rule applies to telephone conversations. It is not uncommon for one party to a lawsuit to record their conversation with another party in the lawsuit; if you have said anything to your spouse or ex-spouse you would not want repeated in the courtroom, you need to let me know about that also.

General Rules

When I am asking you questions, it is called "direct-examination." I must ask questions that are non-leading, and which do not suggest the actual answer. The questions that the other lawyer will ask you are "cross-examination." He may ask you leading questions; that is, questions that suggest answers. When the other lawyer is asking you these questions, he is trying to "put words in your mouth." Leading questions many times begin with "isn't it a fact", "isn't it true that," or similar questions. If you sense that the answer is in the question, be careful. These questions may contain implications that are only partially true and that require an explanation.

Different lawyers have different techniques in cross-examining witnesses. At the outset of the cross-examination, the other attorney may appear to be friendly, but remember that he represents the other side of the lawsuit. Many lawyers, at the outset of cross-examination, are careful not to antagonize the witness so that the witness will prove what appears to be non-controversial information voluntarily and readily. Once this information is obtained, the lawyer will start to ask the harder questions, and press the witness. The moral of this story is that, although the other lawyer may appear to be friendly, he or she is not your friend; be careful that he or she does not lead you into saying something that you do not believe.

Remain calm and polite and do not lose your temper, no matter how hard you may be pressed. Even though something may happen during your testimony that makes you angry or embarrassed, always be courteous to everyone, including the judge, the jury, and particularly the lawyer who is cross-examining you. There are any times in life that it may be appropriate to "talk back" or make some type of wise-crack, but it is never appropriate when you are testifying. Neither judges nor juries like witnesses that appear to be flippant, antagonistic, vindictive, or hostile; this type of behavior can only have an adverse effect on the case. When answering the cross-examining attorney's questions, give him the information in the same tone of voice and manner that you do your own attorney's questions.

For example, a woman would be simply stating the facts and would be an effective witness if she would say, reluctantly, that her husband slept until noon every day. On the other hand, if she were to go on and add that he was a "worthless, shiftless, lazy person who slept every day until noon," her vindictiveness would be very likely to help the cause of her husband.

Never answer a question with a question. For example, if the other lawyer asks you "how old are you?" do not answer with, "how old do you think I am?"

Do not react while the other party, or a witness for the other party, is testifying. You should remain calm, and your expression should not change no matter what the testimony is from the witness stand. No one likes histrionics from a client at a counsel table.

Do not try to memorize what you are going to say in your testimony, either in response to my direct examination, or cross-examination. You will sound coached, and far less believable than if you are simply spontaneous. It is a good idea for you to have a general idea of what you intend to say, but do not worry about saying it exactly the same way every time.

If you have previously been deposed, we will review your deposition testimony before your hearing or trial testimony; but again, do not try to memorize the answers you gave on deposition. You need only to be familiar with what you previously said, and give clear, truthful answers without exaggeration.

At both a hearing and a trial (or at deposition), speak clearly and do not mumble. At a hearing or trial, while you are on the witness stand, look at the members of the jury or at the judge. Talk to them, and speak to them frankly as you would to a neighbor or a friend. Do not cover your mouth with your hand. It is important that you speak loudly enough for everyone in the courtroom to hear you.

Avoid certain expressions like "to tell you the truth," or "I'll tell you the truth," or "to be honest," or "well to be perfectly frank," etc. The judge (or jurors) may be suspicious of witnesses who begin their testimony with these statements. They may believe that a witness who has to keep telling them that something is the truth may not be telling the truth.

Although you and I will discuss the different areas upon which you will be cross-examined, and the types of questions I believe the other lawyer will ask, there will certainly be some questions we have not discussed. If the other lawyer asks you a tough question, do not turn and look to me for the answer. Look him in the eye and answer the questions as truthfully as you can. I will not let the other lawyer abuse you on the witness stand, but I cannot keep him from asking you hard questions, nor can I provide you the answers.

Understand the Question

Everyone is nervous when they testify and nervous people tend not to comprehend things as well when nervous. Do not hesitate to ask the other lawyer to repeat or rephrase the question, as many times as necessary, until you are certain that you have understood it. If you do not believe that you heard the questions correctly, ask the lawyer to repeat it. Once you are certain that you have heard the question correctly and understood it, answer it, but answer only the question that is asked of you and then stop. I do not mean to be evasive; provide the information that is requested but once you have done this, stop talking. Do not provide additional information. You do not testify on cross-examination in order to "tell your story." You testify only to answer the questions asked and, on cross-examination, the best answer to any question is the shortest honest answer. For example, if you are asked how many children are in your family, simply give the number. Do no answer like this: "We have two children. I would have liked many more, but due to the fact that my spouse spent five years in the penitentiary, we were unable to have a larger family." This is what I mean when I say do not volunteer information.

Don't Guess

Many witnesses think that they are supposed to know the answer to every question that is asked. Do not guess at any answer. If you do not know the answer to a question, even though you feel you may appear ignorant or evasive by saying that you do not know, you should nevertheless do so. It is always wrong to guess or estimate.

Be Verbal

As stated above, speak loudly enough so everyone can hear you. Do not nod or make gestures, as these cannot be recorded by the court reporter.

Time and Distance

Be careful with questions involving distances and time. Anytime you estimate distances or time in any of your answers, be sure that you say that it is an estimate.

Quoting Others

When you are testifying about conversations with other people, be sure to make it clear whether you are paraphrasing comments made by you, or the other persons, or whether you are quoting directly what was said.

Never Say Never

Nothing "always happens," and nothing "never happens." Eliminate adjectives and superlatives such as "never" and "always" from your vocabulary when testifying.

Notes, Diaries, Etc.

Do not plan to use any notes, diaries, or any other documents to assist you during your testimony unless you have reviewed them with me. If you refer to notes, etc., during your testimony, the other lawyer will have the right to examine those documents. Use of notes to refresh your memory or any other such documents will allow the other side to examine them.

Questions About Documents

If information is in a document you need to see in order to testify truthfully and accurately, ask the other lawyer to provide you with a copy of that document, if you know that he has it. When confronted with documents, examine them carefully. If you haven't seen a particular document before or did not prepare it, don't try to guess what it means, and don't vouch for its accuracy.

Mistakes

If at any time during your testimony at hearing or at trial, you realize you have made a mistake, correct your answer as soon as you recognize you have made an error.

Listen

Do not let the other attorney put words in your mouth. If necessary, restate or rephrase in your own words the attorney's question. Pay particular attention to introductory clauses preceding questions. Do not accept the other attorney's summary of your testimony unless it is completely accurate.

Is That All There Is?

Beware of questions by the other attorney beginning with works similar to "is that all?" THE OTHER SIDE IS ATTEMPTING TO FREEZE YOUR TESTIMONY. A good answer to such a question would include phrases such as "to the best of my recollection at this time," "that is all I can remember at this time," etc.

Don't Interrupt

Make sure that you allow the other attorney on cross examination, and me on direct, to complete our questions before you begin to answer. If you interrupt the cross-examining attorney, you may be answering a question he is not really even asking, therefore providing him additional information to ask more questions about. If you interrupt my questions to answer a question, it will seem as if we have rehearsed your testimony.

Compound Questions

Often a question will have several parts. For example, "when you talked to Elliot, didn't you say that you were in Dallas, and didn't have time to drive to Tyler to meet with John that afternoon?" It may not be possible to give an accurate answer unless you answer the questions one at a time. In such a case, you may say, "the question has several parts, and I will try to answer each one. When I spoke to

Elliot, I don't believe I told him I was in Dallas. I said it would be difficult to meet with John that afternoon, but I don't believe I told Elliot about meeting John in Tyler." The best way to handle this, however, is to simply tell the other lawyer that he asked you more than one question, and ask him to break the question down for you.

Interruptions by the Other Attorney

Many times, in the heat of battle, the other lawyer may interrupt you while you are trying to answer a question. Let him finish his new question, and say "before I answer that question, I need to finish the answer to the last question." If you haven't finished an answer, that is, if your answer to a question is not complete, you need to say so. Don't count on the judge or the lawyers to know that your answer was cut off.

Demands for Yes and No Answers

While you should never volunteer information on cross-examination, there are times when you need to give an explanation. There are also some questions which cannot be answered with a "yes" or "no" answer. An example is "have you stopped beating your wife?" Obviously, this question cannot be answered by either a year or no answer, because either answer would imply guilt. A short answer setting forth the facts would be called for. Remember that the other lawyer is motivated to make your answers fit his case. Sometimes a lawyer may even try to force your answers to be what he wants to hear. He may try to intimidate you with commands of "just answer 'yes' or 'no'." If you can't answer the question that way, say so. Be prepared to insist that a question cannot be answered with a simple "yes" or "no." Be prepared to insist that the answer requires some explanation. I will be there to help you get a complete answer into the record.

Objections

There will be many objections during the trial. Whenever an objection is made while you are testifying, stop instantly, particularly when I am the one that makes the objection. Do not try to give an answer before the judge rules on the objection. Wait until the judge has ruled. If the objection has been "sustained," the judge believes the objection is correct. If an objection is "overruled," the judge believes the objection is not correct. Do not try to decide what the effect of an objection is on your testimony. When the objection is being made and the judge is giving his ruling, wait silently. After the judge has ruled, either you will be asked another question, or you will be told what to do next.

Whenever the judge tells you something, of course, you will follow his instructions. One common instruction is "please just tell us what you observed, don't tell us what anybody else told you." We will go over these rules before your testimony begins, so don't be concerned about having to learn the rules of evidence. Whatever you need to know at the courthouse, either the judge or I will tell you.

If a question is asked that you do not wish to answer, do not turn to the judge and ask "Judge, do I have to answer that question?" If the question is improper, I will make an objection. If I do not make an objection, answer the question as truthfully and honestly as you can. If there are any questions that you do not want to answer, tell me now, before you give your testimony, so that we can protect you from having to answer any improper question.

Notes to Me

This applies only to clients while others are testifying. During the testimony of someone else, do not tug at my sleeve, whisper in my ear, or give me a nudge. I am trying to concentrate on the testimony, and I cannot listen to that testimony and listen to you at the same time. Simply make a note of what you wanted to tell me and, when the other lawyer's examination of the witness is complete, I will review those notes either at the beginning or at the end of my redirect or cross-examination of that witness.

Talking About Our Preparation

You should never be embarrassed about admitting that you have met with and consulted with me prior to your testimony. If asked what you talked about, simply say that I instructed you to be truthful and honest. The other lawyer may simply ask you "who have you talked to about this case?" What the other lawyer may try to suggest is that some person has prepared you for your testimony, and sometimes he goes even further and suggests someone has told you what answers to give. There in nothing wrong with having spoken to me about your testimony. If you have talked with members of your family, your doctor, your pastor, your counselor, or anyone else, do not be afraid to say so. There is absolutely nothing wrong with talking about your case with other persons, as long as you do not violate the witness role discussed later in this paper. People who say they have never talked to anybody else about their case, or their testimony, usually will not be believed. The important point here is that no one should ever be allowed to tell you what your testimony should be. I will never tell you what evidence to give; I will never tell you to cover the facts in a certain way, or to lie, or to distort the truth. What you and I will discuss before you testify is simply the most effective way in which to tell the truth.

Don't Converse With the Opponent

After testimony at a hearing or at trial, do not chat with the other side or their lawyer.

Don't Speculate

Do not try to figure out before you answer whether a truthful answer will help or hinder our case. Answer truthfully. I can deal with the truth effectively, but I am handicapped when you answer any other way.

The Witness Rule

As witnesses are sworn in at the beginning of their testimony, one of the lawyers will usually "invoke the rule." The rule is also sometimes called the witness rule. The most important thing you need to remember about the rule is that the testimony must be your own. Your testimony must not be affected by the testimony of others. If you are not a party, you must not see or hear the testimony of others. Neither a party nor witnesses may discuss their own testimony or the testimony of others. If the rule has been invoked, the judge will place you under oath and explain the meaning of the rule to you. From that point forward, until the case is over, you may not discuss any facts of the case with any person but me. Only the lawyers in the case will be able to discuss the case with you.

Be Careful

Even though the judge may not formally "place you under the rule" and explain it to you, do not assume that the rule has not been invoked. Always assume that you are under the rule unless I tell you otherwise.

In order to comply with the rule, once the case has begun, do not discuss the facts of the case with anyone but me. Do not discuss the facts of the case with your spouse, or any member of your family, or with anyone that you work with, or with anyone who will or may be a witness in the case. If you are my client, do not discuss the facts with any witness whom we have asked here on your behalf, and do not discuss the facts with any witness who may be appearing for the other side. If you are a witness and have been asked to appear, either by my client or by me, do not discuss the facts with my client. If you are a witness, and the lawyer on the other side asks to speak with you about the facts of this case, the best thing to do from my client's point of view is to decline to speak with him or her unless I am there.

Unfortunately, some people do not follow the rule. If you see or over-hear anyone else discuss the facts of the case, in disobedience of the judge's order, you need to let me know right away. If a witness vio-lates the rule, there can be very serious consequences. The judge, for example, may order the testimony of the defending/offending wit-ness to be "stricken from the record," which means it would be just as though the witness had never testified. Additionally, since it is an order of the court given to you personally, if you disobey that order, the judge can hold you in contempt of court and punish you.

Chapter 19

CHILD CUSTODY BASICS IN TEXAS

I often have potential clients that come into my office wanting "custody." Custody is a term that means different things to different people. In my experience, child custody matters can be one of the most contentious types of family law. In this chapter, I will discuss how custody is determined in Texas.

Issues Related to Children

When parents cannot agree, regarding custody, their case will go to court for a custody determination. Every custody battle will be examined by a judge on a case-by-case basis. The judge will then make a ruling based on your family's unique circumstances and Texas Law.

In Texas when parents can no longer co-parent and seek court intervention, there are four areas that must be addressed in child custody cases handled by a court:

1. Conservatorship

2. Rights and Duties

3. Parenting time / Visitation (Possession and Access)

4. Child Support

Whenever children are involved in a Texas court case, "Best Interest of the Child" is the standard from which decisions must be made. This will address the above four issues.

Texas Family Code Section 153.002 makes it clear that, "the best interest of the child shall always be the primary consideration of the court in determining the issues of conservatorship and possession of and access to the child."

The Best Interest of the Child

One of the most cited cases regarding best interest is the Texas Supreme Court's 1976 decision *Holley v. Adams*. The Court wrote that certain factors to consider in ascertaining the best interest of a child include the following:

1. The desires of the child

2. The emotional and physical needs of the child now and in the future

3. The emotional and physical danger to the child now and in the future

4. The parenting abilities of the individuals seeking custody

5. The programs available to assist those individuals to promote the best interest of the child

6. The plans for the child by these individuals or by the agency seeking custody

7. The stability of the home or proposed placement

8. The acts or omissions of the parent which may indicate that the existing parent-child relationship is not a proper one

9. Any excuse for the acts or omissions of the parent

These are not the only factors a court can consider when making a "best interest" determination. Nevertheless, the *Holley Factors* **provide a framework for analyzing "best interest."**

1. Desires of the child

One of the Holley factors includes the desires of the child. Texas Family Code 153.009 provides on the motion of either party, that a judge must interview a child who is age 12 or older in the judge's chambers to determine the child's wishes.

It is a common misconception that a child age 12 or older will be allowed to decide which parent they get to live with. If the child tells the judge that they want to live with a specific parent, the court can take this into consideration in making a decision but it is not necessarily the deciding factor.

2. Emotional and physical needs of the child, now and in the future

The court may consider the development of the child and how they are likely to benefit from being placed with either parent as a conservator. A child's emotional and physical needs should ideally be satisfied to as near as possible to the child's state prior to divorce.

3. Emotional and physical dangers to a child, now and in the future

Danger to a child can be short-term and/or potentially ongoing, and the court must weigh evidence supporting concerns of either physical or emotionally dangerous conditions surrounding the parents seeking conservatorship and possession and access to the child.

A criminal record, and abuse in particular, can be a major factor in custody determinations. If one parent has a history of abusing the children, they are not likely to be granted any sort of custody, and may even be required to have their visitation with the children be supervised, if they are granted visitation rights at all.

4. Parenting abilities of the parent or individual seeking custody

If one of the parents has consistently taken care of the child's daily physical and emotional needs, and the other parent would not likely

142

perform the same parenting duties to the extent to which the child is accustom, the court will weigh those abilities accordingly. Work and travel schedules can be a factor in assessing which parent has the best parenting abilities.

How each parent interacted with the child in the past, and the degree to which they were involved in the child's life usually has a strong impact on the custody decision. If parental involvement in the child's life was split equally before, the courts will likely want to maintain such a split. If one parent clearly handled all aspects of raising the child before, sole custody will likely be granted to that parent.

5. Programs to help custodial parents foster the best interest of the child

Being an active part of the community where a child lives is important to their sense of self and healthy development. If a child actively participates in local civic, church and sports programs, a court may weigh the evidence of the child's activities in evaluating their best interests, to decide conservatorship and possession and access.

6. Plans for the child by the parents, individuals, or agency seeking custody

When custody and visitation issues are contested, the parties will need to meet with mediators, court-appointed attorneys, and parenting facilitators, to try to work out a parenting plan in the child's best interests. In this process, which could go to hearing and trial in family court, parents identify and write their proposed plans to manage and provide for the mental, emotional, and physical needs of the child.

Parents who are unwilling to cooperate with the other parent or consistently try to undermine and badmouth the other parent in front of the children are less likely to receive custody rights. A parent that shows a willingness to cooperate with the other parent when it comes to visitation and co-parenting will have a stronger case for their custody wishes.

7. Stability in the home and proposed placement location

Generally, if a child is well adjusted in the home where the family resided before the court, and the parent who will continue to reside in that location, is the better parent to be the conservator with sole possession and access, the court will favor a decision that least disrupts the child's daily life. If, however, the current situation is detrimental, and one of the parents seeking custody is moving to a much better living situation with plenty of benefits to the child, the court may consider the evidence of such claims.

The stability of the environment in which each parent lives can have a major impact on custody decisions. If one parent has a fluid or unstable living situation, they are not likely to be granted primary custody.

Courts often lean towards achieving as much continuity for the child as possible. They recognize that change can be incredibly difficult for children to cope with, and they want to keep as many aspects of the child's life the same. Thus, if the child has already been living with one parent full time, or one parent is getting the family home, the court may rule in favor of granting that parent primary custody so the child can maintain continuity.

8. Acts or omissions by a parent indicating an improper parent-child relationship

Abuse and neglect of a child, in any discernible format, is certainly considered by the court, as it would help predict circumstances in the best interest of the child. The failure of a parent to meet a child's mental, emotional, and physical needs, on a temporary or other basis, can be the basis upon which the court determines conservatorship.

9. Excuses for the acts or omissions of a parent seeking custody

There may be temporary conditions a court considers when evaluating options for the placement and custody of a child. If the parent, most likely to be the better conservator, has a temporary condition or issue affecting their ability to carry out parental duties, the court may consider evidence of the temporary nature of such a condition, and information relative to the likelihood of such a condition to reoccur.

Please keep in mind that, with the possible exception of the "best interests of the child" factor, none of the aforementioned factors on their own will be the sole determining reason a court rules one way or another in your custody case. They will always look at all the evidence and make a decision based on the big picture.

Factors that Courts Won't Care About
Previously, it was common in family law to prefer mothers on custody issues. On November 7, 1972, Texas voters approved the Equal Rights Amendment to the Texas Constitution.

As a result, the following issues are no longer considered when deciding custody issues:

1. Infidelity

2. Marital Status

3. Gender

4. Racial Issues

5. Religion

Conservatorship

In Texas, what most people think of as custody is called conservatorship. Chapter 153 of the Texas Family Code sets forth the framework for appointing individuals as conservators and granting rights of possession and access to a child.

There are two types of conservators—Managing and Possessory.

Managing Conservators

Managing conservators are divided into sub-categories—sole managing conservator and joint managing conservator. Under the Texas Family Code, it is presumed that the parents should be named joint managing conservators.

Sole Managing Conservator

A sole managing conservator is a person granted exclusive right to make decisions for the child. In order to avoid joint conservatorship, clients must prove that it is not in the "best interest of the child."

This is usually seen in situations where a parent:

1. Has committed domestic violence against a member of the family

2. Has substance abuse problems

3. Has engaged in behavior that endangers the child

Joint Managing Conservator

A joint managing conservator is one of two people who share the rights and duties of a parent, even if the exclusive right to make certain decisions is awarded to only one person.

Possessory Conservator

A possessory conservator is a person who is designated by the court as having a right to possession of a child under specified conditions, and who is authorized during their periods of possession to exercise certain rights of a parent.

It is a common misconception regarding joint managing conservators that each parent must have equal periods of possession.

For many people, getting a divorce can be difficult. However, when children are involved things can become even more complex. This can be because parents may disagree regarding a parenting plan, decision making, or care of the children. When this happens, the case may have to go to court and a judge will make the decision.

Rights and Duties

In most family cases, a parent of a child whether sole, joint, or a possessory conservator, has the following rights and duties at all times:

1. The right to receive information from any other conservator of the children concerning the health, education, and welfare of the children;

2. The right to confer with the other parent to the extent possible before making a decision concerning the health, education, and welfare of the children;

3. The right of access to medical, dental, psychological, and educational records of the children;

4. The right to consult with a physician, dentist, or psychologist of the children;

5. The right to consult with school officials concerning the children's welfare and educational status, including school activities;

6.   The right to attend school activities;

7.   The right to be designated on the children's records as a person to be notified in case of an emergency;

8.   The right to consent to medical, dental, and surgical treatment during an emergency involving an immediate danger to the health and safety of the children; and

9.   The right to manage the estates of the children to the extent the estates have been created by the parent or the parent's family;

10.   The duty to inform the other conservator of the children in a timely manner of significant information concerning the health, education, and welfare of the children;

11.   The duty to inform the other conservator of the children, if the conservator resides with for at least thirty days, marries, or intends to marry a person who the conservator knows is registered as a sex offender under chapter 62 of the Code of Criminal Procedure or is currently charged with an offense for which on conviction the person would be required to register under that chapter.

In most family cases, a parent also has the following rights and duties:

1.   The duty of care, control, protection, and reasonable discipline of the children;

2.   The duty to support the children, including providing the children with clothing, food, shelter, and medical and dental care not involving an invasive procedure;

3.   The right to consent for the children to medical and dental care not involving an invasive procedure; and

4.   The right to direct the moral and religious training of the

children.

If a parent is named sole managing conservator under Texas Family Code Section 153.074, the parent will have the following rights and duties exclusively (unless limited by the court):

1. The right to designate the primary residence of the child;

2. The right to consent to medical, dental, and surgical treatment involving invasive procedures;

3. The right to consent to psychiatric and psychological treatment;

4. The right to receive and give receipt for periodic payments for the support of the child and to hold or disburse these funds for the benefit of the child;

5. The right to represent the child in legal action and to make other decisions of substantial legal significance concerning the child;

6. The right to consent to marriage and to enlistment in the armed forces of the United States;

7. The right to make decisions concerning the child's education;

8. The right to the services and earnings of the child; and

9. Except when a guardian of the child's estate or a guardian or attorney ad litem has been appointed for the child, the right to act as agent of the child in relation to the child's estate if the child's action is required by the state, the United States, or a foreign government.

However, when parents are appointed Joint Managing Conservators, the court is mandated to allocate these rights duties jointly, exclusively, or independently.

Joint Rights

A joint right is when you can exercise subject to the consent of the other parent. The following rights are almost always made jointly:

1.   Consent to marriage or

2.   Enlistment in the armed services

Independent Rights

An independent right is when either you or the other parent can exercise the right without conferring with each other and neither of you need the other's consent.

The following rights are almost always made independently:

1.   The right to receive information about the children,

2.   The ability to consult with physicians and teachers, and

3.   The right to direct the moral and religious training of the children.

Exclusive Rights

Exclusive rights are when you can exercise the right without conferring with the other parent, do not need the other parent's consent, and the other parent cannot exercise this right at all.

The following rights generally given exclusively to one parent—to receive child support and the right to designate the primary residence of the children.

Parenting Time / Visitation

Part of settling the children issues involves establishing a schedule when the children will spend time with each parent. Under the Texas Family Code, it is presumed to be in the best interest of the child that this schedule be the Texas Standard Possession Schedule. However, parents can agree to do something different.

Standard Possession Order (Parents within 100 Miles of Each Other)

During the Regular School Year

Weekend	Midweek
1st, 3rd, and 5th Weekends Pick up on Friday at 6PM and Return on Sunday at 6 PM	Every Thursday from 6pm – 8pM

Elections During the Regular School Year

Weekend	Midweek
1st, 3rd, and 5th Weekends picking up the children from school on Friday and return to school on Monday.	Every Thursday pick up from school and return to school on Friday.

Some parents make this election because they can have more time with their child. It also allows them to have less interaction with the other parent.

Spring Vacation

In even numbered years, the non-primary parent has the right to possession of the child during spring vacation.

Summer Visitation

The non-primary parent receives the right to have the child for 30 days during summer vacation.

Holidays

Holidays alternate. For example, if the father had the children for thanksgiving then the mother would have the children for Christmas. In the next year, it would be the reverse.

Odd Number Years

Thanksgiving	Christmas	New Years
Mother has the right to possession of children from the time school is dismissed for the thanksgiving holidays until Sunday at 6:00 p.m.	Father has children from time school is dismissed until noon on December 28	Mother has the children from December 28 at noon until 6 p.m. on the day before school resumes after the Christmas vacation.

Even Number Years

Thanksgiving	Christmas	New Years
Father has the right to possession of children from time school is dismissed for the thanksgiving holidays until Sunday at 6:00 p.m.	Mother has children from time school is dismissed until noon on December 28	Father has the children from December 28 at noon until 6 p.m. on the day before school resumes after the Christmas vacation.

Standard Possession Order (Parents over 100 Miles of Each Other)

During the Regular School Year

1. At the option of the non-primary parent they can have regular visitation as described above OR

2. One weekend a month of that parents choosing

3. No Thursday visitation

Spring Vacation

The non-primary parent gets every spring vacation.

Summer visitation

The non-primary parent receives the right to have the child for 42 days during summer vacation.

Holidays

Same as above.

Child Support

Custody includes financial support of the child. The Texas Family Code contains a rebuttable presumption that application of the statutory child support guidelines is in the best interest of children. Under Texas Family Code Section 154.122 guidelines child support is presumed to be in the "best interest of the child."

Child Support usually includes one parent paying child support and providing health insurance for the child

Child support is determined in Texas based on a percentage of the paying parent's net income up to the first $8550/month of income. The parents usually share the uninsured medical expenses between them.

The exact formula for calculating guideline child support is very involved but your estimate as follows:

Net Resources =

1. Monthly Gross Income

2. Less Federal Income Taxes (single, one deduction)

3. Less Union Dues

4. Less Medicare and Social Security Taxes

5. Less Insurance Premiums paid for Children

Support Percentage

Number of Children	Support Percentage
1	20%
2	25%
3	30%
4	35%

If the parent paying child support has no net resources, the court can impute income equal to minimum wage under Texas Family Code Section 154.068.

"In the absence of evidence of a party's resources, as defined by Section 154.062(b), the court shall presume that the party has income equal to the federal minimum wage for a 40–hour week to which the support guidelines may be applied."

How Long is Child Support Paid?

Child support is paid until the minor child turns 18 or still in high school, whichever is longer.

Step Down Provisions

If you have more than one child, the amount of child support will change over time. For example, if you have two children, the parent paying child support will most likely be paying 25% of their net resources as child support. When the first child graduates from high school, the parent would start paying 20% of their net resources as child support.

Sole Discretion of Primary Parent

Child support can be used at the discretion of primary parent. The parent who pays child support has no say on how that money is used.

What if Child Support Payments are not made?

Violation of a child support court order can be dealt with through child support enforcement options, which can include jail time, fines, and garnishment. Some of the options that are used to help insure court ordered child support is paid include:

1. **Wage withholding** – A notice is sent to the parent's employer directing the employer to automatically deduct the amount of support from the parent's wages. The money is then sent to the child support office who distributes it to the child.

2. **Contempt** – If a parent violates a court order to pay child support, the court can hold that parent in contempt. This means the parent can be jailed and placed on community supervision for up to five years. In addition, the parent can be ordered to pay the attorney fees associated with the enforcement.

3. **Money Judgment** – If child support is not paid in a timely manner, the unpaid child support can be reduced to a money judgment that starts to accumulate interest.

4. **License Suspension** – If a parent fails to pay child support for more than 90 days, a court can order the suspension of any license that has been issued to that parent.

Chapter 20

DIVIDING PROPERTY IN A TEXAS DIVORCE

One major issue during a Texas divorce is the division of community property and debts. There are multiple steps that must occur during such a division including:

1. The assets must be identified. This is typically done by completing a sworn inventory.

2. Characterize the property. Before going into characterizing the property, it is crucial to understand that Texas is one of a handful of states that has "community" property.

3. Valuation of assets.

4. Dividing the property.

This article outlines the process of dividing property in a divorce in Texas. Property can either be divided by agreement or by court order.

1. Identifying Assets

The first step in dividing marital property during a divorce is to determine the property that is owned by the spouses whether or not it is community or separate property. The local rules of most Texas counties require each party to file an inventory, appraisement, and proposed division of property prior to the final trial on the merits of a divorce case.

The inventory must list each asset and liability of the marital estate, along with the corresponding value and character. Further, the Inventory should detail and value all claims that could impact the property division, including claims for reimbursement and fraud.

The inventory is then used by the judge to help formulate what a just and right division of property would be for the spouses. Inventories are not only useful in Trial but are also useful during the divorce process for use in negotiations and mediations when attempting to settle the case.

For these reasons, it is important to take all steps necessary to ensure that the Inventory is comprehensive and accurate. This begins at the outset of the case by gathering all relevant documents and information in order to assist in proving the value and character of the marital estate.

2. Characterization of Property

As a Texas Court can only divide the community property of the parties in a dissolution proceeding, the characterization of property as either community or separate is an important second step to the division of marital property in a Texas Divorce.

Separate Property

The Texas Family Code has codified the definition of separate property as follows:

1. The property owned or claimed by the spouse before marriage;

2. The property acquired by the spouse during marriage by gift, device, or descent; and

3. The recovery for personal injuries sustained by the spouse during marriage, except any recovery for loss of earning capacity during marriage.

Community Property

The Texas Family Code and case law define community property as follows:

"Community property consists of the property, other than separate property, acquired by either spouse during marriage."

The distinction between community property and separate property is important because the court divides the community property between the parties but cannot do so for separate property.

Property possessed by either spouse during or on dissolution of marriage is presumed to be community property. To rebut the community property presumption, a party who asserts the separate property claim must present "clear and convincing" evidence of the property's separate character.

3. Valuation of Property

Once an asset is designated as either community or separate property, the parties must prepare to place a value on it. As a general rule, property to be divided in a divorce proceeding should be valued according to its fair market value.

Texas courts must divide the community estate in a manner that results in a just and right division. Before a court can determine whether the division of marital property is "just and right" under Texas law, a value must be placed on each asset.

Often our client's property, assets, and debts include:

1. Closely-held businesses

2. Partnerships

3. Corporations

4. Limited Liability Companies

5. Family trusts

6. Professional practices

7. Advanced degrees

8. Real estate

9. Ranches

10. Securities

11. Livestock

12. Oil wells

13. Overseas holdings

14. Executive compensation packages

15. Estates

16. Student loans

The valuation of community assets can be established by:

1. Agreement of the parties

2. Documentary evidence

3. The testimony of the parties, or

4. The testimony of a qualified expert

In most cases, the value assigned to the assets and liabilities of the marital estate should be determined at of the date of divorce, or a date that is as close to the date of divorce as possible. The court has discretion to determine which valuation dates to use.

Sometimes, valuation of assets may require experts such as:

1. Forensic accountant

2. Real estate appraiser

3. Real estate agent

4. Business appraisers

Forensic Accountant

Forensic accountants are generally used in cases to trace assets in order to prove an asset is separate property or community property. They may also search for undisclosed assets and communicate the significance of certain property or income.

Real Estate Appraiser

If spouses cannot agree on their real property's value, then a spouse can hire a real estate appraiser to give an opinion of value of the property under the current market conditions.

A real estate appraisal involves obtaining the sales price for comparable properties in the area and extrapolating a value for the subject property based on the comparable properties.

Real Estate Agent

Real estate agents can also be used to value real property. Like real estate appraisers, they are knowledgeable about the real estate market and have access to what properties are for sale or have sold for in the properties neighborhood

Business Appraiser or Business Valuator

If you and your spouse own a business, the business will need to be valued and appraised. A business appraiser often does this evaluation. The appraisal will be based on an evaluation that includes:

1. The business records

2. Interviewing the business employees

3. Business inventory

4. Dividing Your Assets – The Just and Right Division

Once the parties have completed their inventories, including all property and debts, then the spouses are in a better position to begin informed settlement discussions or commence a trial on the division of their property.

If the case goes to trial, the standard a court must follow in dividing the community property of the parties is "a just and right manner." This takes into account the rights of each spouse and any children of the marriage.

However, Under Texas case law, a judge has wide discretion in determining what is "just and right." A "just and right" division of the community property could be awards to each spouse of 50% of the community property or a division that grants to one spouse a disproportionate share of the property.

The court considers several factors in making its decision regarding what is a "just and right division" of the community assets and liabilities. These factors include:

1. The length of the marriage

2. Each spouse's level of education

3. Future business opportunities and employability of each spouse

4. The disparity in earning capacities or income

5. The health and physical condition of each spouse

6. The financial conditions and obligations of each spouse

7. The disparity in the ages of the spouses

8. The existence and size of the separate estates of each spouse

9. The nature of the property being divided, including liquidity, income production, and possible tax consequences

10. The existence of children of the marriage

11. Benefits the party not at fault would have derived from the continuation of the marriage

12. Fault in the breakup of the marriage, including claims of fraud on the community

13. Expenses paid to maintain the community estate during the pendency of the case

14. Temporary spousal support paid during the pendency of the case

15. Attorney's fees and costs incurred during the litigation

Chapter 21

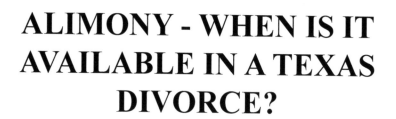

ALIMONY - WHEN IS IT AVAILABLE IN A TEXAS DIVORCE?

This chapter addresses Spousal Support, Spousal Maintenance, and Alimony in Texas and when it is available. A good place to begin this discussion is to define Spousal Support, Spousal Maintenance, and Alimony in Texas.

Temporary Spousal Support

Spousal Support in Texas is awarded on a temporary basis while a divorce suit is pending. It is meant to be temporary spousal support in order to provide a financially dependent spouse with income during the divorce proceedings while the parties are working on a resolution to their financial situation.

Temporary spousal support is based on the common law duty to support one's spouse during the marriage, by providing "necessaries" such as food, clothing, shelter, and medical care. As a result, an award of temporary spousal support can be taken into account when the court divides the spouses' community property, since the spouse who is providing such spousal support is entitled to reimbursement from their community estate.

To be entitled to receive temporary spousal support, the requesting spouse must demonstrate that:

1. The parties have a valid marriage

2. He or she is unable to pay for necessary expenses

3. The other spouse can afford to pay the amount of spousal support sought

If the spouse receiving temporary spousal support remains unable to pay for necessary expenses at the time of the final hearing/trial, he or she should consider requesting spousal maintenance for a period of time after the divorce is granted.

Post-Divorce Spousal Maintenance

Post-Divorce Spousal Maintenance is a relatively new thing in Texas. Until 1997, Texas did not have any law governing spousal support. When the Texas Legislature passed the law, the intent was to keep a spouse off of welfare and from becoming a ward of the state. The Texas legislature revised this law in September of 2011 and changed some of the eligibility rules for court ordered spousal maintenance.

In Texas, spousal maintenance is money that one spouse pays to the ex-spouse for a period of time after the divorce. Post-divorce spousal maintenance is something a family law judge can order a spouse to pay involuntarily depending on if the other spouse meets certain eligibility factors under the Family Code.

Keeping in mind the original intent of the legislature in many cases judges are reluctant to grant an award of spousal maintenance after a divorce. Before a judge will grant an award of post-divorce spousal maintenance the requesting party will:

1. Have to plead for it (ask for it in their pleading filed with the court)

2. Show that they lack property to meet their minimum reasonable needs (In other words, if there is a lot of marital property to be divided such as money in bank accounts, retirement, etc., they are less likely to need spousal support)

3. In most cases, the party asking for post-divorce spousal support will be required to have been married to you for 10 years or longer

4. The requesting party in most cases will need to demonstrate that she/he is unable to earn sufficient income to meet minimal needs

5. The requesting party must demonstrate she/he has made a diligent effort to earn sufficient income or develop

skills to do so

Other reasons a spouse can ask for post-divorce spousal support include:

1. The other spouse has committed family violence

2. The requesting spouse has an incapacitating disability

3. A child of the marriage (of any age) has a physical or mental disability that prevents the spouse who cares for and supervises the child from earning sufficient income.

Duration of Spousal Support

Should an ex-spouse be awarded spousal maintenance, there is generally a cap on how long a judge can award spousal maintenance.

Basis of Award	Length of Marriage	Maximum Duration
Married 10+ years	Between 10 and 20 Years	No more than 5 years
Married 10+ years	Between 20 and 30 Years	No more than 7 years
Married 10+ years	30 Years or more	No more than 10 years
Disabled Spouse	N/A	As long as spouse satisfies eligibility requirements

Disability

If an ex-spouse is awarded maintenance for suffering from an incapacitating disability under the family code, the court can order spousal maintenance to be paid for as long as the spouse continues to satisfy the eligibility requirements under the applicable provisions.

How much Spousal Maintenance

To calculate how much to award in spousal maintenance the court will first determine what an ex-spouse's reasonable needs are. Things that a judge must consider when deciding how much to award in post-divorce spousal maintenance include:

1. The financial resources of each spouse after divorce (including separate property)

2. What effect paying child support or spousal maintenance will have on both spouses' ability to pay their bills

3. One spouse's contribution to the other's education, training, or increased earning power;

4. The age, employment history, earning ability, and physical and emotional condition of the requesting spouse

5. Each spouse's education and employment skills and how long it would take for the spouse asking for maintenance to get education or training

6. Whether either spouse inappropriately spent community funds or disposed of community property during marriage

7. Homemaker contributions

8. Marital misconduct of either spouse

9. Family violence

The court cannot award more than either $5,000 or 20% of the paying party's average gross monthly income, whichever is less.

Contractual Alimony

Another form of post-divorce spousal maintenance in Texas is "contractual maintenance" or "Contractual Alimony." This is voluntary and paid according to an agreement between the spouses as to how much it will be and how long it will last. In this form of post-divorce spousal maintenance, a spouse does not have to prove any legal eligibility requirements.

This is sometimes used as a way to divide up marital assets or for tax purposes. There is no guarantee for contractual maintenance. It is something that would require both parties to be able to come together on an agreement.

Chapter 22

WHAT IS AND WHY DO I NEED TO DO DISCOVERY?

A t some point in the divorce process, there is a good chance your ex will serve you with documents known as Discovery. During our divorce cases, it is not uncommon for us to hear our clients complain about answering discovery requests.

Generally, Texas divorce lawyers do not enjoy the discovery process any more than their clients. However, Discovery serves an important part of the divorce process.

What is the purpose of Discovery?

Although Discovery can be unpleasant during a Texas Divorce, many times it is exactly what your divorce attorney needs to prove your case.

This is because it is your divorce lawyer's job to use the facts of your situation to build your case in order to get you a "just and right division of the property" or get you custody of your children.

It is important to put the effort in at the beginning, as this will allow for more persuasive arguments later in the case during mediation or in court. It is difficult to have a meaningful mediation if we do not know what the property is.

This also will save you money in attorney's fees if we are able settle the case early on in mediation rather than later because we did not do our homework at the beginning.

Discovery

Discovery usually involves one or more of the following documents:

- Request for Production
- Written Interrogatories
- Request for Disclosure

- Requests for Admission

- Sworn Inventory and Appraisement;

- Depositions

Discovery requests contain questions that you must answer and documents that you must produce. You are required by law to respond to these discovery requests.

Request for Production and Inspection

The Request for Production and Inspection contains a list of documents that you must present. This discovery tool is useful because it allows you to ask for just about any document you may want.

Most frequently, requested items are for financial records such as bank accounts, 401(k) plans, stock options, income, gifts to people other than the spouse, safe deposit boxes, telephone records, insurance plans, and credit card statements.

Interrogatories

Interrogatories contain a list of questions that you must answer. Some questions have multiple parts, so please be sure to answer each and every part to each question.

These questions require responses about relevant issues, such as the location of bank accounts, balances in those accounts and signatory privileges on the accounts. Although almost anything relevant to the case can be asked, the total number of questions is limited to 25.

Another thing to consider is that because the questions are limited to 25, you may not want to ask about financial questions unless necessary because that information should be produced through the use of a sworn inventory or the requests for production. These questions are signed under oath.

Rule 194 Requests for Disclosure

The Rule 194 Requests for Disclosure contains a list of standard questions that you must answer in every civil case. The questions require parties to identify persons with information relevant to the case, identify expert witnesses, detail the legal contentions, and specify any economic damages.

How Quickly Must I Answer Discovery Requests?

In most circumstances, once you are served with Discovery requests you have 30 days to respond. However, because preparing the discovery can be a very time consuming process we like to get the rough responses back from our clients within a couple weeks to allow us time to organize formal responses.

Request for Admission

Requests for Admission are statements that the opposing party must either admit or deny. If they fail to respond, they must state a reason why the statements can neither be admitted nor denied.

Once a response is given they are stuck with the answers, and failure to answer them will result in all of the requests being deemed admitted.

Sworn Inventory and Appraisement

This discovery tool is unique to divorce cases. It requires a party to list every asset he or she knows about. The party also has to characterize the assets as either separate property or community property and to place a value on it. This document is signed under oath, so a party who deliberately hides assets will be subject to penalties and remedies from the court.

Depositions or Oral Discovery

Depositions are a form of oral discovery. These are witness examinations taken under oath in front of a court reporter. Any witness with information that will affect the case can be deposed. Under Texas law, the deposition testimony can be presented to the court as if the witness were testifying in person before the court.

Depositions are often times most useful after the other discovery tools have been used. This is because you can then ask questions regarding their responses to prior discovery.

What if I do not Respond?

I have had more than one client tell me that "That it is none of the other party's business!" If the discovery is objectionable, your lawyer will object. However, during the divorce process there are a lot of things that can legally be asked for.

Be advised that your failure to respond to the discovery requests or responding to them late allows the opposing party to request a number of sanctions and penalties against you, including but not limited to payment of fees and the opposing attorney's fees.

Ultimately, responding to discovery is your responsibility. It is not something that your lawyer can do for you.

Chapter 23

WHEN SHOULD YOU GO TO DIVORCE COURT IN TEXAS?

Most of the clients that I represent would prefer to settle their cases outside of court. However, occasionally, my clients or their spouses are insistent on going to court and having a judge hear and decide their case.

They may have a romantic idea that going to court will be like in the movies. When they get there, though, they discover that the courtroom is packed. There are lawyers in the front of the room, waiting for the day to start and the judge to arrive. Some lawyers are stressed, some look bored, and others are relaxed. Behind the wooden gate are the spouses packed into wooden benches who are often confused about what happens next. They wonder how long this will take and no one is happy.

Why do Spouses go to Texas Divorce Court?

Everyone who comes to see me tells me how agreeable and easy their divorce is going to be. If that were true, we could be in and out of the courtroom quickly. Once in front of a judge, it normally takes five minutes or less to prove up an agreed divorce.

Statistically, 90% of all divorce cases settle. However, most Texas divorce cases are not uncontested right from the start, despite what all my consults tell me. I usually tell my consults a couple things:

1. I will let them know if their divorce case is uncontested after it is over.

2. I can get them divorced as fast as the slowest person in the relationship.

Usually after I tell them this, there is a pause. I believe the pause has to do with the realization that it does not matter how agreeable they personally are, because if their spouse is not agreed then their case is not an agreed divorce.

Usually when people come to see me, it is because they are not get-

178

ting along well enough with their spouse to amicably divide up all their property and decide how they will co-parent their children.

Usually when people go to divorce court, it is more involved than just ending their marriage. One of the worst reasons to go to court is because someone wants to fight. When this is the case, someone is angry and upset and wants to punish their spouse. This in turn causes their spouse to be angry and upset, and then want to fight as well.

Some people want to go to court so they can tell the judge their story. They expect justice.

However, these people do not realize that even if they do go to court, they will never be able to tell the judge their story. The judge is not interested in their story. The judge is interested in only certain facts so the judge can make a ruling and get them out of the courtroom.

You Should do a Cost-Benefit Analysis before Looking for Justice in the Courtroom

When I hear potential clients talk about how they want "Justice" or that it is for the principle of the matter, I know there is a problem. "Justice" through a divorce court room is not necessarily what everyone thinks it is.

It makes me think about the lyrics from the musical "Jesus Christ Super Star" when Pontius Pilate says "What is truth? Is truth unchanging law? We both have truths. Are mine the same as Yours?"

When something does not go a person's way in court, you will hear that person talk about how "they got shafted and the judge is corrupt." These people say they want what is fair; however, in their minds they believe fairness means that the judge will side with them.

However, fairness does not necessarily mean the judge will side with you. Through the divorce process, you and your spouse will be encouraged to try and resolve the case outside of court. However, not everyone is able to do this.

There is a legal procedure in place to resolve cases when spouses are unable to agree without intervention. That procedure is to go to court and be heard by the judge. The judge's job is not to do what you think is fair. It is the judge's job is to decide the case and to be the tie breaker.

The judge has a lot of discretion to make decisions. However, there are also laws put in place by our legislature that guide these decisions. It is a judge's job to follow these laws. Sometimes my clients become upset, because they do not like the laws a judge must follow.

An example of this could be regarding child support. In Texas, there are guidelines for child support laws that a judge must follow. I tell my clients if this case goes to court, a judge is going to follow the Texas guidelines for child support laws unless we can explain why it is in the best interest of your child that we deviate from this guideline regarding child support.

However, outside of court, if we can reach an agreement, there are things we can do to make sure we can push your agreement through the court.

Manage your Expectations of what Justice Looks Like

Everyone is the hero of their own story. I believe most judges try and apply the law to the facts they hear in the courtroom and make a decision that is reasonable. However, if you insist on getting your justice from a judge, it may not be what you want or expect.

It may not be what your spouse wants or expects either. You both may be walking away with a decision that you are far unhappier with than if you could have resolved the case outside of court.

You and your spouse are also looking at the case through different lenses. An example of this could be that one spouse has been a stay-at-home parent and is looking at the divorce wondering how they are going to now support themselves. The other spouse is looking at it through the lens of all the money that has been earned by their efforts.

In many of my cases, the two different perspectives clash and result in a fight. For the stay-at-home spouse, they often think that justice does not provide them enough after the divorce. For the other spouse, they often believe that justice provides the stay-at-home spouse too much support. When you add the perspective of the judge to the mix, you can see that the court system is a mixture of many ideas about justice.

Where to get Justice for Your Divorce Case?

Having your divorce settled by a judge in a divorce court, involves some uncertainty. If going to court means you might not get what you want, then why go to divorce court at all?

Two good reasons for going to divorce court in Texas are:

1. To prove up an agreed divorce

2. If you are unable to reach an agreement with your spouse because they are being difficult or unreasonable

Generally, it is better if you can resolve divorce issues in mediation and through negotiation. This is because you and your spouse will craft how your lives will look after the divorce rather than depend on the judge.

Chapter 24

SIX STEPS YOU SHOULD TAKE BEFORE YOU DECIDE TO DIVORCE

There are six things you should do before you act on any thoughts you have about divorce. These steps are specific to Texas divorce, but can be applied to divorce in many states. Here are the top six things to do:

1. Make Sure your Marriage is Over

Before you file for divorce, first make sure your marriage is over. You might want to consider seeking some divorce counseling even if you think there is no hope for the marriage.

You do not have to wait for your spouse to participate before seeking help from a counselor. Your employer, church, friends, or an attorney can provide you with recommendations for a counselor who may be able to help you and your spouse.

2. Get Legal Advice from a Texas Divorce Lawyer

Even if you never end up hiring a Texas divorce lawyer to handle your divorce, we highly recommend you meet with one and gather as much information as you can before you even discuss divorce with your spouse.

The divorce laws in Texas are a lot more complex than people realize. Even what many people believe to be a very simple process can be very confusing to families already in distress. One reason why seeking legal advice sooner rather than later is that the actions you take now may very well affect your life during the divorce as well as the outcome of your divorce.

The following true story is an example of why this is important. One of our clients decided that he wanted to save money by not hiring a divorce lawyer. He thought his matter was simple, and he and his wife would agree on everything. It turned out his wife did not like his offer, and she hired a divorce lawyer. The divorce lawyer set the case for a hearing and got the man kicked out of his house and got the wife spousal support.

The man then hired us to represent him in the divorce. We were able to help him get a fair settlement for the divorce, and he did not have to pay spousal support after the divorce. Unfortunately, he was stuck with the outcome from the hearing while divorce was ongoing— something that could have been easily prevented had he been represented from the beginning.

It is important to understand your options ahead of time not wait until after the divorce process has started. It is often easier to prevent something then it is to fix something after the fact.

3. Talk to an Attorney Before You Move out of the Marital Home

I am often asked by the people I meet with whether or not they can move out of the marital home. There is generally no one right answer that fits every circumstance. Generally, before advising someone, I want to know more about their life situation including:

1. Has there been domestic violence?

2. Are there children involved?

3. Do you want to be able to stay in the home during the divorce?

4. Do you have financial concerns and can you afford it?

5. Do you want to use any of the property currently in the home?

6. Will moving out affect your financial interest in the property?

7. Are there emotional considerations?

Some things to consider when making a decision to leave your home include:

1. If you leave the house, you may not be able to return after a court hearing

2. Having to pay for an additional residence can be expensive

3. If your children are living in the marital home this may limit your access them

4. If You Have had an Affair, Talk to a Lawyer Before You Talk to your Spouse or Anyone Else

Generally, in Texas all financial matters will need to be disclosed to your spouse during a divorce. However, you do not have to go out of your way to let your spouse know that you have been having an affair. In fact, the admission of an affair to your spouse would be admissible in court and possibly can have dire consequences.

Texas is a no-fault divorce *state, which essentially means that neither party necessarily has to prove the other spouse did anything wrong in order to get a divorce. The main reason why adultery matters in a divorce is that if adultery can be proven, it can be used to support a request from the spouse not at fault for a disproportionate division of the* community property *between the parties.*

This means any illicit sex with someone other than your spouse could end up costing you thousands of dollars.

5. Safeguard Your Assets and Start Discussing Divorce with your Spouse

It is important for you to take precautions or possession of certain assets during a divorce such as:

1. Pictures, family heirlooms, other sentimental objects

2. Vehicles

3. Valuables stored in safes such as cash, gold, or gems

4. Money in bank accounts that might be liquidated by your spouse

In addition to securing the above items from your spouse, if you plan to file for divorce, you can ask your attorney to also ask for a Temporary Restraining Order, which will prohibit your spouse from transferring or otherwise disposing of any property covered by the restraining order.

6. Prepare Financially before you Start Discussing Divorce with your Spouse

Other protective measures you might consider in your divorce planning include:

1. Protect your own credit rating by freezing or closing joint cards and by blocking or removing your spouse's access to other joint credit such as a home equity loan.

2. Open a separate bank account in only your own name.

3. Change the name on utilities, phones, and any other bills with which your spouse might make problems.

4. Pay down joint bills first, marital property next, and your own separate property last.

Chapter 25

DO NOT MAKE THIS
DECISION BY YOURSELF!

I hope that this book has given you a better understanding of what to expect and how to protect your right to get fair treatment. I hope you have been introduced to enough concepts and legal principles to picture your future and how to begin navigating toward success. Thank you for investing your time with me.

I'd like to return the favor and offer you something in kind. Normally, I charge clients $350 an hour for my time. However, if you call my office and mention that you've read this book, I would be happy to waive that charge and provide an initial consultation for free.

You've experienced uncertainty, sadness, and frustration. Allow me to help restore your peace of mind. Knowledge is power. With my help, you can gain the knowledge to take back control and shape the future you deserve.

Please call my team now at (281) 717-6711 to schedule your consultation. I am looking forward to helping you put the past behind you and enjoy a brighter and more hopeful future.

Take action today toward

YOUR NEW FUTURE!

Call our office today:

Make your appointment for a

FREE CONSULTATION

(a $350 value)

CALL:

(281) 717-6711

OR VISIT:

WWW.BRYANFAGAN.COM

ABOUT THE AUTHOR:

Bryan Fagan, Esq.

Author Bryan Fagan has always had the inclination to help others and he always put forth all efforts in everything he has set out to do. Coming from a real estate background, Bryan felt his real passion was in helping families.

This passion continued into his career as a Texas licensed attorney whose law practice focuses exclusively on divorce and family law. Mr. Fagan is a member in good standing with the State Bar of Texas, Houston Bar Association, and The Woodlands Bar Association.

Mr. Fagan is the founding attorney of the Law Office of Bryan Fagan—a Texas boutique family law firm located north of Houston. His vision is to establish a unique law firm, one singularly focused on the clients' experiences when dealing with difficult and often intensely emotional legal matters involving divorce and family law. As evidenced by so many glowing testimonials, clients benefit tremendously from the firm's exclusive family law and divorce representation with a focus on customer service.

Since its formation, the Law Office of Bryan Fagan has earned the trust of clients in cases ranging from relatively simple divorces to those involving complex property divisions, contested child custody issues, parental visitation matters, and child relocation disputes.

Bryan Fagan was born in Denver, Colorado and raised here in the Houston area. He loves his now home state of Texas where he mentors and counsels families dealing with tough legal issues. When he is not working, mentoring, counseling, and writing books, the author spends his free time working out at the gym, attending church, and spending time with his family and friends.

Made in the USA
Columbia, SC
26 March 2018